HOW I WON THE VICTORIA CROSS

D1860451

Owing to the antiquity and rarity of this book, certain pages are regrettably absent, and readability is compromised due to the blurring of the original text. If you possess any insights regarding the availability of these missing sections, kindly inform us. Your assistance is crucial in ensuring the completion of this significant work for the benefit of future generations.

HOW I WON THE VICTORIA CROSS.

BY

T. HENRY KAVANAGH, ESQ.

GYAN

Published by

GYAN

Gyan Publishing House
5, Ansari Road
Daryaganj, New Delhi-110002
Phone: 011-47034999, 9811692060
E-mail: books@gyanbooks.com

Distribution Network
gyanbooks.com
India, USA, Canada, UK, Australia

© Publisher

All rights reserved. No part of this work may be reproduced, stored, adapted, or transmitted in any form or by any means, electronic, mechanical, photocopying, micro-filming, recording or otherwise, or translated in any language, without the prior written permission of the copyright owner and the publisher.

ISBN: 978-93-6208-106-3 (PB)
First Published, 1860

2nd Impression 2024

Printed at: Gyan Press, Delhi.

The book is sold subject to the condition that it shall not, by way of trade or otherwise, be lent, resold, hired out, or otherwise circulated without the prior publisher's written consent.

HOW I WON THE VICTORIA CROSS
Author: T. HENRY KAVANAGH

LUCKNOW KAVANAGH IN HIS DISGUISE.

HOW I WON THE VICTORIA CROSS.

BY

T. HENRY KAVANAGH, ESQ.

ASSISTANT COMMISSIONER IN OUDH.

"What is it that you would impart to me?
If it be aught towards the general good,
Set honor in one eye, and death i' the other,
And I will look on both indifferently:
For, let the gods so speed me, as I love
The name of honor more than I fear death."

JULIUS CÆSAR, *Act I.*

LONDON:
WARD & LOCK, 158, FLEET STREET.

1860.

PREFACE.

I RETURNED to Europe, after an absence of thirty years, to gratify a strong desire to see the place of my nativity; to refreshen the head and heart in a land beautiful to look on, and abounding in intelligence; to educate my children, and to restore the health of my wife. I reached London, unconscious of owning a single friend in that prodigious metropolis; and, had it not been for the fame that preceded me, I might have returned to the East unknown and uncared for.

The Government did little to honor me; but, in private society, the generous remembrance of my devotion everywhere obtained for me the kind notice of my countrymen, English, Irish, and Scotch; whose approbation is more precious than official distinctions. These may be got for acts not known by the public, but public praise is only awarded to public merit.

Why not write a book? I was repeatedly asked; but feeling unequal to the task I would not attempt it. At last I was persuaded to write; and this volume is humbly sent forth as the best I can do. It is not intended as a work on the war, of which I have said only as much as was needed to elucidate my share in the great struggle to suppress the Mutiny.

I fear that many of the noble fellows whom I followed into action will think me forgetful of their merits. I inserted many names and many deeds, which were struck out as only likely to please the parties themselves; and, to satisfy the present taste, I had to free the work from details that involved the mention of many persons.

Very few artistic attempts have been made to embellish the work, and there are scarcely any disquisitions to tire the reader. It is, in short, a very simple book, remarkable principally for the extraordinary adventures of the author. It is a strange story, written by a plain man, who, moved by the spirit of his noble companions, endeavoured to do his duty at a time when courage and devotion were needed to preserve the empire of the East.

INTRODUCTION.

THAT marvellous country of the East: The seat of the earliest of mankind: The source from whence language and learning have flowed to enlighten and ennoble the West. That land which filled the mind of the European with visions of riches—of beauty—of romance—of voluptuousness. The land of vast plains—stupendous mountains—wild and magnificent forests—gigantic rivers, rolling tumultuously down to the sea—inhabited by curious people! You were too grand not to excite the enterprising spirit of Europeans, who are ever craving for adventure, and thirsting for knowledge.

They came—they trafficked—grew rich, and presumptuous. They stood beside the dark man towering in strength and intelligence. They saw his weakness; and the profits of commerce were succeeded by a desire for conquest. They warred—vanquished—seized the fairest provinces with gigantic strides, did those wicked men of the West; and in two centuries they were paramount throughout the empire of the Moghul.

'Tis the destiny of the civilised to subdue and enlighten the barbarous: the Anglo-Saxon had been selected for the work.

Misrule and oppression—cruelty and corruption—rapacity and tyranny, were now displaced by a *spirit* of justice and indulgence—honesty and charity—and, after awhile, by generous and forbearing rulers, who, if not always right, deserve, at least, the credit of meaning to be so. Marauding armies of soldiers, and rapacious officials, no longer traversed the empire year after year, and the people were instructed that there are rights and duties which all good governments respect and enforce.

Trade expanded to a size unknown before, and spread almost untaxed and wholly unmolested. The agriculturist saw waste lands brought under the plough, by the construction of canals, and by a greater demand for its produce. In short, peace and plenty were beginning to reign in that glorious empire of the East, where disorder and dissention existed before; and its children would have grown great under the miraculous light of the West. They were imbibing that knowledge which is the sinew and marrow of the European, and patience—a little patience—and our strength would have been their strength. Miserable wretches! they did not understand the astounding grandeur of the nation which meant to prepare them for emancipation and for self-government.

Foreign rule is perpetuated by the respect of the subjected. Alas! after two hundred years we were still without it. The white and the black men are dissimilar as day and night. There is no communion of feeling, and little of thought. The European, conscious of his superiority, is proud and disdainful, and spurns the advances of the dark man. He applauds by silence, and upbraids with a loud voice. He is feared by every one and loved by few. The white man arrogantly dwells in a strange land as if it was his, unmindful that force subdues but cannot attach a people; which is the only security for peace and prosperity. Europeans in India know little of the country in which they dwell, and less of the peculiarities of the people. Haughtiness alike alienates the wise and the simple; and this was one of the stimulating causes of the troubles of 1857.

There was, I repeat, a spirit of justice. No government was ever actuated by better intentions, or had more talented servants. But it made the mistake, (and will go on doing so till another rebellion,) of endeavouring to govern an immense empire by very few and almost irresponsible subordinates. There was too much to do, and nobody to complain if imperfectly done; and the close of every year saw most of the administrators, great and small, blowing their own trumpets. There was no public opinion to warn the indolent, and none to encourage the clever and the industrious; official praise and dispraise were not independent. Therefore, business was slow in all things. Worst of all, there was too little supervision; and, as a matter of course, shameful corruption in the native subordinates, who, being poorly paid and remorselessly overworked, seized every opportunity of selling their services. It is no exaggeration to say that the people oftener looked to them for the disposal of their suits, than to the European officer, who, sometimes for the want of zeal and ability, and often from the want of leisure, was unable to purify his Court.

Justice was indeed slow, expensive, and uncertain; and our officers almost inaccessible. In all things the interest of the State was considered to be of greater importance than the welfare of the people, who were, almost without exception, treated as rogues and liars. This was another cause of the discontent of 1857.

The Army of India was composed of the most able-bodied and most bigoted of Asiatics, and we had for many years endeavoured to increase their pride, in the belief that it would make them better soldiers. Step by step we put them, in imagination at least, over ourselves, and they came to know that we were few and far between, by the spread of information from our own lips, and through our own Press. Their conceit was intolerable, and, little by little, they were alienated from the officers, whose confidence was such, that they did not care to learn the conduct and characters of the men; and, like their civil brethren, were capricious in rewarding. It is a strong expression, but it is quite true, that in the course of time, the Native Army was feared. Its proportions had grown great—its courage unquestionable—and its temper excitable, when the thoughtless issue of GREASED CARTRIDGES unexpectedly provoked it to Mutiny.

It is not always that mutiny and rebellion are productive of social and administrative reforms based upon principles previously declared to be dangerous to an empire. Many of the official traditions of India, like our dwellings, have been burnt, never we hope to revive again. A fanatic army fought for its conscience, and ignorant peasants against the foreigner: without disturbing their mighty masters they uprooted long-cherished theories and systems founded on ignorance and impudence.

Opinions once obstinately defended and enforced are now unowned and unhonored; officials who prided themselves on their superior tact are silent, for astounding events have depreciated, if they have not wholly extinguished, their policy and their conceited knowledge.

The whole system was weak and profitless, as are all administrations founded on selfishness. By a miracle we acquired, and by chance we governed, enormous provinces. European energy and enterprize which have marvellously developed the resources of the western world lay dormant in the East. There it is a business of profit and pleasure—here Europeans are paid servants who have no interest in the progress of an antagonistic race. With small means and little earnestness they hoped to benefit and instruct millions and millions of beings. With a feebleness peculiar to Englishmen in the East they labored languidly on the surface, and helplessly gazed at the prodigious wealth around them. While industriously laboring elsewhere to upturn hidden wealth, here they were content to receive a stipulated hire.

A rebellion has aroused them to activity, and every department has its projects of improvement. Instead of devising schemes of revenge for shedding innocent blood, and destroying an enormous amount of public property, the European has grandly turned on himself, and is busy correcting his own faults. It is of no avail! The house that needs a thousand brooms cannot be swept by fifty: the gem of the East cannot be shaped and polished by the present number of artificers. Its lustre is obscured by the dust of ages, and it is certain that we have too few, and possibly too little time to cleanse it. A tendency to discord and disorder is the chronic condition of India: its heterogeneousness; the social reforms which civilization is there timidly forcing upon ignorance; the antagonism that exists between the white and the black men; the offensive exclusiveness which Europeans will continue towards Indians, are some of the causes which will always endanger the peace and prosperity of India.

The infusion of knowledge would certainly benefit the people, and assuredly endanger the European. England considers that

India is hers, not alone for her aggrandisement, but for the prosperity and enlightenment of the people. She is to give in exchange for the products of the East, the virtues of the West: she is to stay there till the people are able to govern themselves. A prodigious and a magnanimous task, which two hundred monitors and two hundred missionaries have gone to accomplish!

The social enlightenment of the natives is impossible unless the rule of the Anglo-Saxon is perpetuated by colonization. Committees have been formed, and persons examined, and their suggestions rejected as impracticable. If the official records of India were searched many precious things would be found which were first neglected as impossible, and adopted by another generation with complete success. It is the misfortune of India that there nothing is treated as possible. Should the convulsions of man not expel us before, the statesmen of the next century will think of us with contempt for rejecting a legitimate and, indeed, the only effectual means of imparting the knowledge and prosperity of Europe to the gentle and intelligent people of the East. It is not easy to do, but it can be done, and should be done, at all hazards, to some extent. There is plenty of room for another race, and that other the most active and industrious of mankind. What does it signify, even if it is true, that the white man would deteriorate in the land of the black man? Deterioration would be the work of many ages, and it could only be physical: it is intellectual and not physical power that is to be introduced. I have said elsewhere that the education of the people of India can only be effected through themselves; and if we socially plant Europeans among them, a grand source of reaching them will be provided. The barrier of caste is more fictious than real, and whenever we familiarly mix with the people it will be trodden down.

Europeans at present know little of the natives, and that modicum is derived from the low and the litigious. The upper and middle classes are only officially brought into contact with Europeans, and our opinion of them is formed from the conduct of menials. There is one stereotyped idea of native character which almost every European adopts, without investigation: it is the one which the early adventurers had when they plundered and oppressed them to retire to sumptuous homes in England—it is the same that still quickens the arm, the leg, and the tongue of Europeans on the slightest provocation. Indians may approve the honest and impartial principles set forth in our laws and our literature, but ourselves they cannot appreciate till colonization mingles and discloses the qualities of the two races. Many thoughtlessly assert that familiar intercourse is impossible; which is only true of the proud men who now reside among them: the admixture of races begins from below, and not with the higher classes. Others aver that Indians are incapable of moral culture; which is a monstrous untruth: the sources of education come from abroad, and for centuries the people of India have been debarred communication with the rest of the world, and corrupted by misrule and oppression.

HOW I WON THE VICTORIA CROSS.

CHAPTER I.

Englishmen not easily frightened, and disregarded first signs of Mutiny—Sir Henry Lawrence came to Oudh—Nana of Bithoor nearly rode over me—Troops in Oudh excited by placards—Irregular and regular troops mutiny at Lucknow—Night ride alone to the conflict—An *émeute* of the citizens suppressed by Captain Carnegie—Residency defences began and indifferently done—Volunteers ought to be better than regular troops when better educated—Military Police mutinied, and were attacked by Thornhill, M'Rae, and two noble Puthans—Executions did no good, and in my opinion never will.

During the months of February and March, 1857, symptoms of disaffection were manifested by the Native Army, who peremptorily refused to use the Enfield cartridge, which they believed to be dipped in grease—a Hindoo abomination. But those signs of discontent were insufficient to alarm Englishmen, whose confidence in themselves is supreme, and may be said, indeed, to be sublime.

Europeans in the East occupied so lofty a position, that they disregarded these early signs of the approaching crisis, and considered them merely as ridiculous indications of religious fervour, which would soon vanish of themselves. They saw nothing that they had ever done to provoke hostility. Theirs was a just and a generous rule. Were there not Courts of Law to redress wrongs, and to punish crime; had not property increased; was it not protected to an unprecedented degree; and were they not doing everything in their power to produce increased prosperity? Indeed, if any one had cause to be dissatisfied, it was the European, who felt that he was gradually losing the supremacy which he everywhere considers to be his birth-right.

So the Anglo-Saxon reasoned, and fearlessly pursued his usual course, quite confident that he could speedily trample out mutiny and rebellion in any form. He is a noble creature; but it is a pity that he lives so isolated from the people of India that it will always require violent demonstrations of disaffection to awake him to a sense of danger. He there regards popular feeling as unstable; and public wrongs as altogether unfounded. Because he means to be just and generous, he thinks that he is so.

At that time my family was staying at Cawnpoor, and it was arranged that it should remain there till the end of the summer, as there was some difficulty in procuring a suitable house at Lucknow. But Providence willed that my wife should differ with friends under the same roof, which changed her plans, and saved my family from the massacre. We confidently looked forward to spending the hot weather in a house adjoining the Chutter Munzil Palace, on the River Goompty: our minds were wholly undisturbed by the occurrences at Berampoor and Barrackpoor, which did not seem to forbode trouble.

Sir Henry Lawrence succeeded Mr. C. C. Jackson as Chief Commissioner of Oudh, and his presence inspired confidence. The rumour of a conspiracy against the Europeans was dissipated by assurances, from the officials intrusted with the investigation, that the extensive circulation of wheaten cakes in the North Western Provinces, and in Oudh, was an innocent trick to alarm the Government. Up to the end of April, the only persons affected by these omens were the authorities. They did little, however, to appease the fears of the soldiery, who industriously communicated to each other the absurd report that we meant to convert them to Christianity.

The Nana of Bithoor came over to Lucknow in April, and some persons have supposed that he was then engaged in fomenting the spirit of discontent among the troops. It is doubtful, for his bearing and that of his followers was always arrogant, and it was only the subsequent events which gave their vulgarity the appearance of design. He was himself greatly irritated at the denial of the rights he claimed from the Government as the adopted son of Bajeerao; but this did not make any apparent difference in his demeanour towards Europeans, to whom he was as courteous as an ill-bred man could be.

I saw him once, when he visited Sir Henry Lawrence; and again, one evening while I was walking homeward, when he and his cavalcade nearly rode over me, as we suddenly met under the large masonry gateway leading to the Teree Kothee. To save myself, I threw out my arms, and their horses shyed and alarmed the Nana, who was nearly pitched from his handsome Shekawattee. I am not one of those who think that a dark skin justifies rudeness, and I would have stepped aside if I could have done so, for at that time there was no reason to suspect the atrocious part he was to take in the tragedy of

Cawnpoor. The monster is said to have died, but the public may be sure that the Government of India will not relax in its efforts to capture him till it is in possession of the most indubitable proofs of his demise.

No one dreamed of the coming struggle for supremacy between the white and the dark man, till the ferocious deeds of May, 1857, at Meerut and Delhi, warned us of the immensity of our danger. Successful attempts were now made to excite the religious prejudices of the troops in Oudh. Placards, couched in the most vehement terms, spread the wildest rumours of our designs; and reminded the people of the perfidious annexation of Oudh, and of some real and imaginary wrongs. Most of these imflammatory papers were posted by Mahomedans, who rejoiced at the opportunity offered for a return to that state of disorder and violence for which they have an especial liking. The city of Lucknow abounded in reprobates, whom peace and quiet impoverished, and they did their utmost to inflame the aversion which most natives have to Europeans.

The murder, at Meerut, of a near relative of my wife, so frightened and distressed her, that I yielded to her entreaties to abandon our new house for a couple of rooms in the Post Office, near the Residency, and we remained in one of them to the end of the siege. Soon after, the public treasure was transferred to the Baillie Guard, and some of Her Majesty's 32nd Foot occupied the Banquetting Hall. The civil and military families gradually removed into buildings adjoining. But many civilians misunderstood the extent of their danger, and I had trouble to induce them to leave their homes in the city, and only succeeded in persuading a few to prepare for a siege by purchasing simple necessaries.

The irregular troops at Lucknow could dissemble no longer. The 7th Regiment mutinied, and it was hoped that the prompt measures of Sir Henry Lawrence, on that occasion, would have preserved us from the mutiny of the regular troops, which happened on the 30th of May. He did all that was possible, at that early date, to meet the danger, which he at one time thought conciliation might arrest. No human efforts, however, could have saved us on that night, but for the interposition of Providence. At the Residency, we could not have resisted more than a few hours, for we had no place to retire to more secure than the roofs of the houses, to which the women and children instinctively flew on the report of the first gun in the Mureon cantonment. There they looked with awe towards the city for the dreaded rising of the people, and trembled as they saw the burning buildings, and heard the roll of musketry and the loud booming of artillery in the distance.

On the night of the 30th of May there were three hundred men of the 32nd Foot, and some European artillery, in the cantonments, to oppose three regiments of infantry, and one of cavalry, who might be joined by the irregular regiments at the Moosa Bagh and the Dilaram. I was anxious to share in the struggle which we fancied was taking place at Mureon, and was the first to reach Sir Henry Lawrence from the Residency, with the comforting assurance that there were no signs of the anticipated rising among the citizens. I found him acting wholly on the defensive, which was the most prudent course owing to the darkness of the night and uncertainty as to the extent of the mutiny. He was affected by the ruin which he now saw was inevitable. He was without fear for himself, and his noble nature melted at the thought of the danger in which we were soon to be involved. A more unselfish man never breathed, and he only trembled for the fate of others. He would willingly have walked to death to avert the doom that threatened his countrymen, and his nervousness was wholly owing to the feeble state of his health, and to the generous pulsations of as fine a heart as ever beat in a manly breast. The screams of the mutineers in their lines—their figures gliding across the streets, firing the empty thatched bungalows around us—the lurid glare of the fierce flames—the crackling of the burning bamboos—and the noise of the falling roofs, resembling distant guns—aroused serious thoughts of the appalling trial foreboded. Encompassed, as he thought we should be, by a multitude of enemies, what wonder if a mind borne down by disease, and fatigued by the cares of State, bent under so great a weight.

It was in the subsequent proceedings of the mutineers that Providence befriended us. They hastily retreated from Lucknow towards morning, instead of entering the city, where they would doubtless have been aided by thousands of vagabonds who lived on the vices of the people, and panted for the destruction of a power which preserved the weak from the lawless. These sorry creatures expected to be joined by the troops, and could not forbear showing their feelings, even after the dastardly course taken by the mutineers. But they were more cowardly than the Sepoys, and a small military demonstration, conducted by our indefatigable city magistrate, Captain J. Carnegie, soon extinguished their zeal for the present.

I returned to the Residency at about two o'clock

at night, passing the office of Mons. Depratt, who had prepared the roof of his building for defence—so little was then known of the character of the war we were soon to be engaged in—leaving the whole of the lower floor open! Mr. Rees, (who published a most interesting narrative of the defence,) and some Siekhs were with him, and I was challenged. While Sir Henry Lawrence was pursuing the mutineers, the late Major Banks, Captain J. Carnegie, and myself, were engaged at the vacant barracks of the 32nd Foot, on the hazardous duty of disarming a large guard, who tightly clutched their muskets as we took them away, and demurred at what they conceived to be an unmerited dishonour. The task was performed with great temper and discretion by those two officers, who were men of no ordinary courage and decision.

Active preparations were now made for the defence of the dilapidated old Castle known as the Muchee Bohawun, and those insignificant fortifications which we were to defend for nearly five months, were languidly commenced. Men who have never been in war know little of its wants, and some of the most remarkable errors in our works remained undiscovered till the fire of the enemy drove us from our guns. The Chief Commissioner best comprehended what was required. Major J. Anderson and the other Engineers, especially Captains Fulton, Anderson, and Innes, cheerfully endured all kinds of fatigue and exposure to complete the defences. If their inexperience of war occasioned defects and deficiencies, they amply made up for it, during the defence, by their intelligence, and by exertions unsurpassed by any other branch of the service.

At the beginning of June I formed the civilians into three garrisons in the office buildings, and with the assent of the members, nominated commanders to each. At first, room was refused; and it was not till I had personally urged their case upon Mr. Gubbins and Mr. Ommanny, that they were provided with accommodation for their families. Jealousy, and disappointment in the quality of the room provided, sometimes provoked disagreements; for there was a mingling of several adverse elements too close and too sudden to be agreeable to the proud Knights of the Quill. I had less trouble in forming them for military duty than was expected, because most of them were intelligent and good tempered, and had a just conception of the important part they were to take in the approaching defence. Arms were supplied to them, though some persons ridiculed the idea of their being able to use them, and facetiously enjoined the volunteers to be very careful that they did not go off! I, as chief of the class, felt personally concerned in their future reputation, and, to enforce some military discipline, posted sentries, who were relieved every hour. I frequently visited them, and was deprived of rest for several nights, to the injury of my health. Till the work was taken from my hands, on the occupation of the Residency by the military, I perseveringly did all that a civilian could do to form the "uncovenanted" into an efficient body, although a few thought me too officious, and one of them ungratefully rebelled against my authority. The whole body afterwards distinguished themselves by their courage and endurance, and their superior intelligence made them as good, if not better, than regular troops, for the kind of warfare they were engaged in. Precise military instruction is not so essential for fighting behind defences as it is on the open plain, where the drilled soldier would, for a time, be superior to volunteers. No troops go into action with the precision of a parade, although great efforts are made to do it; and those who argue for the superiority of regular troops, should remember that a common soldier's share in an engagement is very simple. It is enough if the commanders of volunteer troops are trained leaders, for those below do as they are ordered, and educated men are certainly better able to follow instructions. Should the volunteer companies of England ever be engaged, such is the effect of education, that they would soon be regarded as equal to, if not, (and I am inclined to think they would be,) superior to the regular army.

On the 12th of June, the military police at Lucknow mutinied, and quitted the station with their arms; and towards evening a requisition reached me, through Mr. Gubbins, to collect as many volunteers as possible. We hurriedly mounted upon artillery horses, and joined in the pursuit of the mutineers, who were overtaken marching towards Cawnpoor. After a harmless fire of shot, grape, and shrapnell, and a feeble charge by the native cavalry, we marched back with a few prisoners, and very little glory.

Messrs. Thornhill, of the Civil Service, and James M'Rae, Civil Engineer, and two Puthans, were the only persons who distinguished themselves in that pursuit. The first impetuously attacked a stalwart Sepoy, who, favoured by Mr. Thornhill's unmanageable mare, ran his bayonet through the skin of the chest into the left arm, and would, doubtless, have killed him, but for the arrival of M'Rae, who disabled the soldier by a sabre cut on the head. The Puthans afterwards, *alone*, charged into the retreating mutineers, and were killed.

During the pursuit, I induced some of the mutineers to surrender, and incurred the displeasure of the late Major Banks and Mr. George Couper, Secretary to the Chief Commissioner, because I resisted their being killed on the spot. To my mind, indiscriminate slaughter was highly injudicious at that stage of the mutiny; and the argument that the mutineers had "done their best to kill us," could not apply to the men who surrendered. It was very doubtful whether severity, even at the first indication of a mutiny among the Sepoys, would have prevented what happened; for one of the most blind, most fierce, and inextinguishable passions of man had been provoked. In fact, each victim to the law excited, rather than intimidated, the delinquents.

Those persons who witnessed the executions before the gate of the Muchee Bohawun Castle, at Lucknow, will recollect the exhortations addressed by the culprits to the crowd, to remember that they were about to die for their faith; and the curses hurled at us, coupled with the menace, that their unmerited end would be avenged by their children, and children's children! The eager multitude, who gazed at the white faces, and at the expiring victims, were not insensible to those appeals, which added bitterness to that vindictive fanaticism which is all the stronger for being unreasonable. Unusually severe punishments are only justified by the end attainable; and it might have been seen in June, 1857, that active hatred against us would be the effect of the executions, which the gentle heart and good judgment of Sir Henry Lawrence limited more than some of his councillors approved.

CHAPTER II.

Civil and military officers die at their posts—Nearly shot by refugees from Seetapoor massacre—Volunteers sent to rescue Europeans at Secrora—Captain H. Forbes a good soldier—Civilians drilled, and Captain R. P. Anderson is rebuked for laughing at them—Martiniere school boys saved—Captain Radcliffe and volunteer horse—Remember the brave!—The volunteers fine fellows—Cawnpoor—Mutineers chase us back to our defences from Chinut.

BEFORE the middle of June, British authority was extinct throughout the Province of Oudh, notwithstanding the generous exertions of our Chief, and the many valuable lives sacrificed to stem the torrent of rebellion. We were daily distressed by news of the murder of some, and of the flight of other Europeans, who wandered through a hostile people, uncertain whither to turn for refuge. Never have Britons shewn such devotion to duty as was evinced in that unnatural war. As long as there was a vestige of submission to their authority, the civil and military officers stayed at their posts, and several perished with their families rather than retire. Englishmen identified themselves with the Government, and every one rightly thought then that on *his* conduct depended the safety of the empire.

The mutiny at Seetapoor occurred on the 6th of June, and the following day a party of volunteers and

Siekh cavalry, under the orders of Captain H. Forbes, were sent out to escort into Lucknow the Europeans flying from the massacre. After proceeding a few miles, we learnt from a traveller of their approach, and I rode on to assure them of their safety. As I galloped eagerly into the mangoe grove, Major Kemble was on the point of ordering the escort to fire, when he perceived that I was a friend, and their alarm was succeeded by intense joy. Captain Forbes, with his cavalry, soon joined us, and while waiting for conveyances for the women and children, I induced several to drink from my flask of brandy, for they had travelled about fifty miles under an awful sun, and were greatly fatigued.

A few days later I was again asked by Mr. Gubbins to take out volunteers with Captain H. Forbes, who was going to bring in the European families from Secrora, where a mutiny was expected every moment. Mr. F. D. Lucas accompanied him. As we neared Nawabgunj, the advanced vidette saw a horseman precipitately retire from the front; and our commander, thinking that the cavalry had already mutinied, drew up on a plain to the right of the road, where we waited for more than an hour. We then advanced, till we reached a magnificent grove of trees close to the town, where over a hundred native cavalry were standing, with horses saddled. Captain Forbes thought them to be a part of his own regiment whom he had called into Lucknow; but their attitude was threatening, and the slightest indiscretion would have provoked a quarrel against great odds, for, including the Siekhs, we only mustered about thirty-five. Captain Forbes behaved with admirable tact, and we passed on to the police station. The chief native officer gave us refreshments while we rested for a couple of hours, (after a ride of twenty miles,) in the midst of about a hundred and fifty armed policemen of doubtful fidelity. The intemperance of a volunteer, who struck and abused one of the police, at one time endangered us; but I pacified the man, who patiently submitted to a very unprovoked assault. Returning to the side of Captain Forbes, the horse ridden by Mr. Lucas kicked me severely, and the vicious beast, at a well five miles further on, where we stopped to drink, bit that gentleman so savagely, that he had to be sent back with two of the volunteers to Lucknow. I shot the infuriated animal to prevent further injury. We were much vexed at losing so spirited a companion as Mr. Lucas, who remained disabled for several days, when he would have given worlds to be up and doing.

After a journey of forty miles we reached Ramnuggur, a town within a few miles of the river Gogra. Here we learnt, by a note delivered to Captain Forbes, from Major Boileau at Secrora, that he did not despair of preserving his regiment from the general contagion. This intelligence caused the former to decide that it would be better for us to return to Lucknow, as the presence of the volunteers in Secrora might alarm the native troops, and precipitate a mutiny before the European families were withdrawn; or, if we thought six of us too few to travel forty miles through a disturbed country, to stay at Ramnuggur till he came back. The volunteers respectfully remonstrated against being deprived of the honour of sharing the danger which seemed to be inevitable on his attempting to withdraw the families; and I made the proposal of attempting to overawe the troops by suddenly seizing the guns. But the excellent judgment of Captain Forbes saw that it was no time for a rashness which might imperil the lives we were going to rescue; and that the object of his expedition would be better effected without us. After giving me a few lines to satisfy the authorities at Lucknow that we had done our duty, he started with his small party of Siekhs, to perish as we feared; and we turned our faces homewards, greatly disheartened by his decision. The soldierly and gentlemanly bearing of Captain Forbes was such, that we felt sure that everything which courage and temper could effect would be accomplished; and a few days afterwards we had the satisfaction of seeing him enter our poor defences with several women and children, whom he had brought away just in time.

To the middle of June, the civilians had been provided with muskets, and some with swords and pistols: now they were regularly embodied into infantry and cavalry, and some were told off to the guns. Captain R. P. Anderson, in his unpretending narrative of the defence, jestingly mentions the drillings to which they cheerfully submitted twice a day; and it is pleasant to know that this body of respectable and intelligent men were afterwards more distinguished for gallantry than he will ever be for witticisms. Although attached to the cavalry, I attended the infantry and artillery drilling, thinking that the cavalry would be of no use should we be besieged, albeit that extraordinary opinions were expressed of its probable usefulness. So little, indeed, was the nature of the approaching struggle understood, that it was seriously proposed to employ horse artillery, up this and down that road, to keep our defences clear of assailants, and I incurred displeasure for remarking that the progress of the defences was retarded by such misplaced confidence. It was once seriously decided to fortify the chief police stations in the city, and to defend those posts with volunteers and native policemen; and I was afterwards asked, through Mr. George Couper, to call for *eight* volunteers to occupy the Martiniere College, which is two miles from the Residency, to assist the masters and boys to defend it in case of an attack. Only six men could be got to join in so mad a project, and the boys were withdrawn to a building inside the defences.

As another instance of our ignorance, I may mention that we began to fortify our positions as if they were to be separately defended, and to attack each other; and it was Sir Henry Lawrence who tore down those superfluous works as soon as he saw them. Most persons inexperienced in war, which cannot be learned from books, would have done no better; and it is really no reproach to confess that we were bewildered, whatever the engineers may now say of having "completed a fortification which turned every house to advantage, and secured as much flanking defence as possible."*

Captain Radcliffe, of the 7th Light Cavalry, commanded the Volunteer Horse, composed of uncovenanted civilians, and a few officers belonging to corps that had mutinied. Lieutenant Warner, a very intelligent and gallant young soldier, was the Adjutant; and Mr. Alexander Bryson was Serjeant-Major of the troop. An extraordinary attachment sprang up between Captain Radcliffe and the civilians, who would have done anything for him. His patient endurance of hard

* See Captain George Hutchinson's badly written "Narrative of the Mutinies of Oudh."

labour, and his conspicuous bearing in action, fully justified this. Brother volunteers, give him praise wherever you go; and, Englishmen, honour the widow and children of so good and gallant a soldier. Valour is plentiful among British soldiers, but valour like his, which was combined with patience, charity, and gentleness, is rare.

The troop made good progress in mounted drill, and in the use of the sword; and when the mutineers began to assemble at Nawabgunj Burabunkee, about twenty miles east of Lucknow, Captain Radcliffe frequently took it into the country to collect information. The first occasion will be remembered by all who survive, for the right good glee with which we stood on the road at Chinut, singing comic and martial songs with noisy choruses, whilst the rain poured down in torrents, damping everything but our spirits. Few of those joyous hearts are now throbbing in this world, and the rest are dispersed, never again to be united. With what glee you stood, wet, and ancle deep in mud, pouring out the lightsome sounds of your voices in songs of Britons' might and England's glory, regardless of danger! Well might the leader be fond of the daring men who sported around him on that dark and stormy night, as he saw each smiling face by the lightning flashed upon it!

Tidings occasionally reached us of the contest going on, at Cawnpoor, between the mutineers and the garrison of Sir Hugh Wheeler. The prevailing opinion was that he would succeed in defending his post till the arrival of relief, which, promised by successive telegrams, was too sanguinely expected before he sought shelter inside that miserable fortification. Their urgent appeals for assistance deeply affected us, and threatening as was our own position, we would gladly have gone to their rescue. It was once seriously discussed, and only abandoned upon a review of the difficulties which our small numbers could not have surmounted.

At last the distressing news came to Lucknow that the garrison, after imprudently capitulating to the Nana of Bithoor, had been mercilessly slaughtered. The heads of our women reeled, and their hearts sickened, as the harrowing story was told amidst the curses and fierce resolves of the men. Many a savage vow was made then, which was awfully fulfilled on the bodies of our enemies, and CAWNPOOR was afterwards the war-whoop for atrocities which the British soldier will disown in the next generation.

The news of this frightful massacre was followed by information that the mutineers of Oudh were assembling at Nawabgunj Barabunkee, with the avowed intention of advancing immediately upon Lucknow; of which, I think, we were rather too dubious. Appalling as was the intelligence that came from every quarter, and impending as was our own danger, the conviction of our true position came slowly, slowly, slowly, till the 30th of June, when the disasterous battle of Chinut brought the enemy triumphantly treading on our heels, as we precipitately and sadly ran to the protection of our defences.

My health had some days previously been fast yielding to fatigue and exposure, and the efforts made to keep up my strength at so critical a time completely prostrated me, so that when Bryson warned me for duty on the fatal morning of Chinut I was too ill to rise. The volunteer troop of cavalry greatly distinguished itself both during the action, and when covering the retreat of the little force of Sir Henry Lawrence back to the defences; which it entered angry, fatigued, and disheartened, through the residue of the garrison, who looked on alarmed and astonished. The spirit of the defenders instantly sank, and the prowess of the victorious mutineers assumed unmerited importance in their eyes.

CHAPTER III.

Confusion within doors and without—Sick and helpless—Nothing to eat from the Commissariat—Thanks for kindness—Get worse health—Everybody makes a noise—Frenzied by glory—The works of nature most charming—Great people will let little folks walk to fame through the Vale of Death—Affairs improve and the defenders are cheerful—Mr. Alexander Bryson, my brother-in-law, a hero, and his wife and children paupers.

I ROSE sick from my bed, and went out to help in the defence, with a vague idea of the extent of the disaster. I found every one in motion, and confused by a feeling which looked like fear. Gates were rapidly being shut—doors closed—barricades constructed—walls loop-holed—guns rolled into position. Surprise and wonder were depicted on almost every face. The suddenness of the assault, and the disgrace it followed, bewildered all. I sat on a cot, (near what was always called our defences, but was only a thin wall five feet high,) with my face buried in my hands, unable to ask any questions, and fretting at my helplessness when action was so much needed. The force of the sun and my excited feelings soon drove me back to my bed burning with fever. Within doors there was the same commotion. Clothes and furniture were being dragged from room to room—women squabbled for the safest places, distracted by screaming children—loud orders seemed to come from everyone, and masters and mistresses screamed for servants, who were fast deserting them. Before the fighting began, accommodation was apportioned to families according to their respective positions in life; that is to say, the greatest lady had the most airy and comfortable room; but, when the enemy's artillery and musketry poured in their shot and shell, those places did not always prove the safest, and nearly all changed their residences without distinction—for danger is a great leveller. We were fortunate in the selection of a room early in May, and several women and children occupied it.

For two days I could be little attended to, for every one was too absorbed by the wants and the dangers around them, and the thoughts of the women were distracted by the terrific roar of musketry and artillery, and by the near patter of balls and bullets. I sank into a state of langour, and when the fits of feverish delirium were off, did nothing but grieve at the condition to which I was reduced. No one but my distressed wife thought of me, and she too was constantly frightened from my side, for fear of the children, who unconsciously ran into danger.

A general alarm prevailed in the garrison. For a week few persons received their rations. There was no method in the issue, and many knew not that food was being served out by the Commissariat. The provisions I had fortunately put by were now drawn upon by the families near us, and by my servants. I had, besides, a couple of cows, which I ventured to bring from outside the defences on the second night of the siege, and their milk afforded sustenance to several infants when their mothers' strength began to fail. We endeavoured in all things to maintain a character for kindness among our fellow-sufferers, and in return we experienced it from many when kindness was greatly needed. I am glad to have an opportunity of expressing our grateful remembrance of those precious favours. To Ensign James May* I am especially indebted, for, when I began to recover, he did his utmost to procure such food as was suited for an invalid.

An attack of erysipelas in the left leg, from the foot to the hip, aggravated my case, and I lay for days insensible to everything but pain. The awful noise of artillery close to the door increased my distress; for every shot shook me, and the poor women and children seemed to forget my existence, as they ran screaming from corner to corner to avoid the shots that penetrated the rooms.

By the middle of July there was little hope of my recovery, and my fond wife had a sad prospect before her. She was unremitting in her care of me, and I was indebted to her devotion, and to Dr. Greenhow's skill and attention, for a change for the better by the 20th of the month. But a new danger threatened me now, of a kind beyond the cure of the doctor. An intense eagerness to know all that went on in the defences seized upon my mind, which every attack, and every success, affected almost to frenzy. Good and gallant deeds have always greatly touched me; and the news of the first sortie—in which a couple of guns were spiked by *three* men against great odds—filled my heart with such violent emotions that it would have burst, had not

* This young gentleman served in the Artillery as a volunteer, and made himself extremely useful in serving the guns and mortars. He was of great assistance to the Chief Artillery Officer in giving the bearings of the enemy's position with the aid of the prismatic compass; he prepared plans for the relief, and for the capture of Lucknow, when he was also employed, occasionally, on the dangerous duty of guiding the troops.

Mr. Dorrett forcibly leant on my chest to keep down its convulsions. As these rapturous fits might bring on a relapse of sickness, I was kept in ignorance of the incidents of the defence for a few days, till I could bear being carried into the verandah, where I insisted upon going after so long and so painful a confinement. Oh! how charming are the works of nature, which neither time nor the violence of man can obliterate. I surveyed the sky and the green fields from my seat, like one restored to sight, and silently offered up thanks to the Almighty that I had lived to gaze on his works once more, and to take my allotted part in that prodigious struggle, which, to my great joy, was not yet over.

The period, I thought, had arrived when I might earn a character for devotion to duty equal to that of others. I had always striven to be a good servant, but my assiduity and impetuosity were attributed to selfish ambition, and I gained no credit for my exertions. After more than twenty years of toil, my spirits sank at the the miserable prospect of a life of drudgery, under the eye of a service that slowly, very slowly, recognised any merit not its own. Reader, you may blame the spirit that rejoiced at a revolution which opened a broad field for fair play, if you have never labored under a despotic rule; but I could not, and did not, attempt to conceal the pleasure which the contemplation of the future now afforded; and I resolved to die in the struggle rather than survive it with no better fame than I took into it. Some persons are born with moderate desires, and others with high aspirations, which they endeavour to realize; and he who walks in a straight course to the pinnacle of his hopes the world will applaud—when he has got there.

When I retired to my sick chamber, at the beginning of the month, all was confusion, and success was doubtful: when I issued from it, after the severe fight of the 20th July, in which the defenders fought all day with signal valour, all was cheerfulness and confidence. It pleased me to look on their gallant faces, as they passed to and fro in their clay-stained dresses, with hopeful greetings for each other. I never tired of listening to the stories of singular daring that several of the garrison were daily performing, and more and more longed for the recovery of my strength, to bear a share of their dangerous duty.

I have before mentioned that Mr. Alexander Bryson was Serjeant Major of the Volunteer Cavalry, for which office his experience and intelligence, and his manly bearing, made him the best fitted of the troop. Many who were in the Upper Provinces of India will doubtless remember the lively and handsome young artist who took their likenesses. He grew tired of this occupation, which often separated him from his family for half a year at a time, and I induced him to accept service in Oudh, where his talents and industrious habits were sure to advance his fortune.

When the mutineers attacked our position he was removed by Captain M'Cabe from the garrison in which I had placed him, to a more exposed post, where the utmost vigilance and daring were needed to resist the frequent assaults of the enemy. On the ninth day of the defence a weak point was discovered that ought to be barricaded. It was without shelter from the fire of the enemy, who were strongly posted in lofty houses only forty paces off, and the duty was so dangerous that Captain M'Cabe could scarce appeal to the members of the garrison to execute it. In the coming darkness lay the only chance of escaping death. Bryson, feeling that the honour of his garrison was concerned, went out to the point referred to, and, under a heavy fire of musketry, which his exposed position at once attracted, finished the barricade; but, as he descended, a bullet pierced his head, and he fell dead to the ground. Bryson's services were so conspicuous that he obtained honourable mention in the report of the defence of Lucknow, and his widow received from the Government a pension of *thirty-six pounds a-year!* He left three sons, who are being educated from the funds collected for the relief of the sufferers by the mutiny in India, and it is thus to the benevolence of the public that they are indebted for support and education, which the Government grant of £19 a-year would not have afforded, except in a station of life for which their excellent father was not reared.

CHAPTER IV.

Sir Henry Lawrence one of the few good men in India—His charity, endurance, and earnest honesty—The garrison of Lucknow preserved by his forethought—May God have mercy on him who tried to do his duty.

THE death of Sir Henry Lawrence on the fourth day of the siege, is known to all who have taken any interest in the affairs of India. We, who knew him personally, will never cease to grieve for him. The State lost an able and most devoted servant, and the public a great friend and benefactor.

I knew him first in 1841, in which year he was assistant to Sir George Clerk, the Political Agent of the Siekh States, whose ability, activity, and prudence, at a very critical stage of our relations with the Lahore Durbar, obtained for him the reputation he has since maintained. I was a clerk in his office, and daily saw Sir Henry, who was then an impetuous and indefatigable officer, and so wholly absorbed by public duties that he neglected his person, and left himself scarcely any time for recreation. He had little of that gentleness of temper which afterwards grew upon him, and, although very accessible, was not always agreeable to natives. He was rather impatient, and not so practical a philanthropist as he subsequently became. A good straightforward native gentleman was sure to be treated with courtesy, and with a cordiality that filled him with pleasure; but woe to the intriguer or deceiver—these, Captain Lawrence met with a stern aspect, and sent sneaking away in fear and trembling. His brusque manner, grotesque appearance, and shrewd sharp look, attracted the notice of strangers at once, who always left him impressed with the feeling that he was no ordinary man. His mind and body were always in a state of tension, and both were alike denied proper rest.

When the Punjab was annexed to the British dominions, in 1849, he very kindly offered me the appointment of head clerk in the Revenue and General Department of the Board of Administration; which I accepted, glad to be once more under an officer who knew how to encourage merit. In spirit, and in heart, he was as chivalrous as ever; and, in addition to the respect and honor which his talents, his honesty, and his great earnestness had earned, he was now revered as the founder and supporter of the Asylum in the Hills for Soldiers' Children. He was somewhat less careless of dress, but not a whit more chary about the time devoted to public business. Indeed, his great indifference to health and comfort was destroying his constitution. The vigour which I thought his mind had lost, was not lost, but fused into his noble heart. He abhorred and perseveringly resisted the spoliation of the upper class of Indians; for, unlike most civilians, he would not make the the interests of the subject subservient to the policy of the Government. His was a broad, capacious understanding, unsuited for the minutæ of an extensive province, and he bent under the weight of the prodigious correspondence on mere matters of detail, for which the training and experience of Sir John Lawrence were better fitted. He quitted the Province because he in vain opposed the severe policy pursued by his brother.

On the annexation of the fertile province of Oudh, in February, 1856, I was appointed Superintendent of the office of the Chief Commissioner, and here I again met Sir Henry. His policy towards the natives of India was known to be conciliatory, impartial, and generous; and he was, therefore, especially selected for Lucknow, where the benefit of his presence among the mean but haughty nobles was immediately felt, and the citizens gladdened by the visits of a man who actively studied their welfare, and encouraged them by frequent words of advice and kindness.

When the civilians were embodied into infantry and cavalry, two of the latter were daily attached to Sir Henry as orderlies. On the 26th of June, I was one of these, and followed his carriage to the Old Castle, where, mounting his favourite white horse, *Ludakee*, he minutely inspected the works in progress, stopping once to observe some officers and civilians who were being taught gun drill. While here, a letter was put into his hands, and dismounting to rest on the edge of a well, he read aloud intelligence from Major Raikes, that Delhi had been captured by the British troops: which was, of course, believed at the time.

Sir Henry was then weak and careworn, and it was easy to see that he was over exerting his attenuated and exhausted frame. With failing health he strove to fulfil the hopes of the Government, but, alas! the feeble tenement which the cares of State had sadly reduced, could not endure the wear and tear to which his active and restless spirit subjected it; and, when the empire begàn to be convulsed by the great struggle for supremacy, his body rapidly yielded, and his great mind collapsed. I sorrowed, as I looked on the deep and drooping furrows of his intelligent face, and thought, on that morning, that the coming severe trial would hurry him to the grave. I was not in a position to be admitted to the intimacy of Sir Henry Lawrence, but my heart was open to the influence of goodness, and I loved and revered him for his noble qualities, which I had many opportunities of observing. To err is the destiny of all men, but it is reserved for noble natures like his to confess errors, and correct them. His faults were few indeed, and arose chiefly from impetuosity of temper, and never from the faintest depravity of heart, for his was transparently pure.

I saw him thrice afterwards, when he was visiting our posts in the dead of the night, attracting as little notice as possible, except when he stopped to admonish neglect, and suggest improvement. I was soon after fastened to my bed by sickness, and saw no more his manly face.

As he lay in the agonies of death, his thoughts were of us; and the instructions he then dictated for our guidance during the defence, evinced his wisdom and anxiety for our welfare. They were recorded in a diary by Major Banks, (an active and clever officer who soon followed him), and the book was recovered by me on the capture of Lucknow, in March, 1858. The following is a copy of his injunctions:—

"I. Reserve fire; check all wall firing.

"II. Carefully register ammunition in store for guns and

small arms. Carefully register daily expenditure, as far as possible.

"III. Spare the precious health of Europeans, in every possible way, from shot and sun.

"IV. Organize working parties for night labour.

"V. Entrench—entrench—entrench—erect traverses; cut off enemy's fire.

"VI. Turn every horse out of the entrenchment except enough for four guns. Keep Sir Henry Lawrence's horse, Ludakee—it is a gift to his nephew, George Lawrence.

"VII. Use the State prisoners as a means of getting in supplies; by gentle means, if possible, or by threats.

"VIII. Enrol every servant as bildar or carrier of earth. Pay liberally—double—quadruple.

"IX. Turn out every native who will not work, save menials, who have more than abundant labour.

"X. Write daily to Allahabad or Agra.

"XI. Sir Henry Lawrence's servants to receive one year's pay; they are to work for any other gentlemen who want them, or they may leave, if they prefer to do so.

"XII. Take an immediate inventory of all natives, so as to know who can be used as bildars, etc.

"XIII. Take an immediate inventory of all supplies and food, etc. Take daily average of expenditure.

"XIV. Put on my tomb only this—'HERE LIES HENRY LAWRENCE, WHO TRIED TO DO HIS DUTY. MAY GOD HAVE MERCY ON HIM.'"

The effect of these instructions was felt to the end of the defence, and to his foresight in furnishing the garrison we owe our salvation. *May God have mercy upon him*, was his own humble and affecting prayer, for he DID HIS DUTY.

CHAPTER V.

Stores of English merchants plundered, and private supplies squandered—Cholera, fever, and small-pox—Garland and M'Grennan save me—A wretched hospital—Sisters of charity, Polehampton, Barbor, Birch, Gall, Parry, Erith, Alone, and a good soldier's wife—The Report of the Defence not impartial—Captain M'Cabe—Under Arrest—A good soldier killed in his fourth sortie—Lieutenant Bonham, gentle, skillful, and devoted—Look out—Processions of the enemy—Jolly companions every one—Bad rhymes, but good verses.

THE dying injunctions of Sir Henry Lawrence, and the care of Captain James of the Commissariat, preserved and husbanded our public supplies. But private stores were wastefully used, especially the stimulants which would have sustained the sick and wounded afterwards. In all the stages of life it is remarkable how few bring the requirements of the future into their calculations, and how little the mind is startled by prospective dangers. "Sufficient for the day is the evil thereof," was well exemplified during the first sixty days of the siege. English provisions, which had been stored by the merchants Depratt, Sinclair, and Johannes, were remorselessly plundered, regardless of the morrow; and, whilst anything dainty lasted, it was greedily consumed. "Let us live and be merry," was the exclamation of some; and scarcely any had the remotest suspicion that a time was coming when we were to repent our prodigality.

Besides the calamities of war, cholera, fever, and small-pox, about the end of July, began to lessen our ranks, and to destroy our children. At one time, there was three young ones lying near me suffering from the latter infectious disease, and I feared it would affect me before I could leave my bed of sickness. Four days' illness killed our youngest daughter, and we were in great anxiety for the others, whom it was impossible to keep away from the diseased children. We encouraged our children to play in the open air, exposed to the fire of the enemy, rather than remain in our pestilential quarters; and, by the mercy of Providence, they enjoyed better health, in consequence, than most of the youngsters in the garrison.

On the 4th of August I ventured to leave my own quarters to visit some friends, and to show myself to my immediate superior. I was that day rescued from death by Messrs. Garland and M'Grennan, while tottering by their post towards the hospital. I had unconsciously got under a fatal fire from Johannes' house outside the entrenchment, when they warned me of my danger and kindly supported me into their quarters. The hard-working and kind-hearted Garland is dead; but M'Grennan is again at his post earning the good will of his superiors by his assiduity and respectability. The Government of India awarded a sum of money* to him for rescuing the records of the Office of the Chief Commissioner of Oudh from destruction, which he effected, at great trouble and discomfort to himself, when the Residency defences were abandoned.

By a safer road I found my way to the wounded civilians whom I was anxious to relieve. What a dis-

* One hundred pounds.

tressing sight was there! The upper galleries of the hospital were almost deserted, being exposed to the shot of the enemy. The rooms on the ground floor were low, dark, narrow, ill-ventilated, and unbearable from the stench of sloughing wounds and other causes, and could not be cleaned as often as necessary. The servants had deserted, and no one could be spared from duty. At this time I saw none of the ladies whose attentions to the suffering afterwards earned them special mention in the Report of the Defence; but I was eye-witness to the gentle and assiduous care of a young cheerful woman, the wife of a Serjeant-Major, whose soothing kindness has found no voice in the memories of her superiors.* I frequently visited the hospital afterwards, with nourishment for persons whom I knew, and on those occasions I saw Mesdames Polehampton, Barbor, Birch, and Gall, generously waiting upon the wounded, and sometimes reading to them. But I also saw Mesdames Parry, Erith, and Alone, at the bedsides of the sufferers feeding them with porridge cooked by themselves. These ladies, too, have found no one generous enough to record their compassionate services. The Defence of Lucknow was an event which ought to have induced an impartial record.

I urged Captain M'Cabe, of the 32nd Foot, (who commanded at the Post Office Garrison,) to allow me to take my turn of duty, but he smiled as he surveyed my trembling figure, and resisted my entreaties. The alarm of an attack one night drew me out at last, and fancying that I saw some of the enemy, I fired without orders, and was rebuked by Captain M'Cabe, who was in the end provoked to put me under arrest. The

* I do not remember the good creature's name.

following day I was released. Captain M'Cabe will be remembered for his incessant watchfulness; his fiery courage, which shrunk from no danger; and his coolness and discretion under fire, which perceived and overcame all difficulties. His spirit and promptitude especially fitted him for the most hazardous sorties. He survived three of them, but was mortally wounded in the fourth by a discharge of grape from a battery, into which he was gallantly leading his party. The Service thus lost a soldier whose intrepidity first brought him to notice in the ranks during Lord Gough's campaign against the Siekhs. He was an honour to his regiment, rough and rugged as were his manners.

I soon begun to take my turn of duty. The guns and mortars were my especial favourites, and I stuck so close to them while yet weak, that my hearing was injured by their incessant roar. I hoped to secure the management of the mortars on a vacancy occurring, but there were others, with more right to that honour, and quite as much zeal as myself, who coveted that distinguished duty, and it consequently never fell to me. In all sieges, excepting in making and resisting assaults, musketry does little execution, and our extraordinary success against the hordes who surrounded us, is attributable to the perfection of the artillery, and the zeal of the officers, soldiers, and volunteers of that arm. Lieut. Bonham was most conspicuous at our post; his gentle temper, skill, and devoted attention to the guns, even when sick and wounded, won for him the admiration of the whole garrison.

When not defending the walls from an attack, our principal duty was to sit on the roof of our dwelling, protected by a thin earthen parapet, and observe the enemy in a street running parallel to the Kaisur Bagh, along which the guards passed to relieve the besiegers. As the native chiefs resided in the direction of the Palace, all extraordinary movement of troops was thus known to us at once. We relieved each other every two hours, and recorded in a book whatever was remarkable. The assaults were usually made in the day, and were always preceded by constant reports from the look-out, like this:—"A large body of infantry, with six standards, gone from left to right.—A long line of matchlock-men, with numerous green and red colours, gone in the same direction,—in all about six thousand.—About five hundred cavalry, regular and irregular, preceded by drums, apparently escorting men of rank mounted on elephants; swordsmen mixed with bowmen following for about ten minutes.—Two brass guns, seemingly twelve-pounders, drawn by bullocks, and escorted by infantry and cavalry went by at a trot—two small horse artillery guns, and waggons, pulled by bullocks.—A small party of regular cavalry, some in grey uniform, escorting a man of consequence, preceded by drums and two standards.—Several doolies.—More infantry and matchlock-men in irregular order, and a long line of running swordsmen and archers."

The look-out, although an excessively hot and unsafe place, was a point of intense attraction on these occasions, and some authority had to be exerted to keep all the curious off the roof, over the parapet of which it was dangerous to lift your head.

The enemy, after the assaults, invariably returned home in the same order, followed by the wounded on litters; but the infantry, matchlock-men, and swordsmen, no longer walked with head erect, chest puffed out, arms stiffly swinging to and fro. Nor did the cavalry plunge and caracole, nor the dark, slim, Pasee* caper and stretch his bow, as he glibly followed in the wake of his discomfited compatriots. To us, in the distance, the whole procession, there and back again, resembled a pantomimic display. But they always left us to bemoan the death of some fine fellows, who had nobly borne their share in repelling the onslault.

We usually had a few days' relief after these great processions, when the look-out was rather monotonous. We spent some of the time there in reading, composing satirical rhymes reflecting on the idle and selfish, and scratching caricatures of each other upon the walls at the top of the staircase: where we took shelter from rain and sun, when nothing remarkable was happening. The duties and dangers of war attracted us to each other, and loosened our thoughts and actions from the bonds of conventionality, so that a pleasant feeling of brotherhood existed at our important post. We bore the twits and fancies of each other with temper, and many a joyous moment have we passed together amidst the patter of bullets, the bursting of shells, and the accompaniments of noise, dust, and smoke.

I hope, dear friends, that the same hearty and charitable spirit will actuate you wherever and whenever you may meet again. Your gallantry maintained the British character for courage, devotion, and endurance: may God grant that the hopeful smiles, which cheered you in the hour of want and peril, may illumine your hearts and smooth your course to the end of life.

The following rhymes, written in pencil on the walls

---

* A low caste of natives in Oudh, who are expert bowmen, and incorrigible rogues.

of the stairs, were suggested by the sentiments breathed by those young spirits, and, very indifferent as they are, I bequeath them to the public as the only fruit of idleness which I have preserved.

All honor to those,
Who, encompassed by foes,
Grew stronger in courage and might:
All honor to them,
Who, like brave Englishmen,
Are ready, aye ready, to fight!

All hail to the dead,
Who by treachery fled
From husbands, from parents, from friends.
There are brave hearts still here
Who your memory revere,
And will trample the heads of the fiends!

You wretches without,
Who go sneaking about,
A terror to none but the weak,
Beware of the wrath
Which your acts have brought forth—
'Tis the vengeance of Britons you seek!

Think not that your babes
Shall redden our blades,
Or their mothers have reason to care;
For an Englishman's pride—
It is known far and wide—
Is the innocent always to spare.

The aged he'll respect,
And the feeble protect,
And the simple he'll pass them with scorn;
But the vicious—ah! they
Shall remember the day
That an Englishman's vengeance was born.

CHAPTER VI.

The spirit of the garrison fluctuates—Servants despair and run away—Fidelity of Natives inexplicable—Good servants badly treated—Wounded in the Cawnpoor battery—Mr. Gubbins unfairly abused—Innes's garrison saved by civilians—Captain Waterman wounded, and is run after by a frightened man—The famous Redan Battery—The 32nd Foot—Good troops and better officers—Sir John Inglis earned his honours—Kind, gentle, patient, generous woman—Captain Fulton, the ablest man of the garrison, not sufficiently praised.

TOWARDS the end of August and beginning of September, the spirit of the garrison fluctuated between hope and despair, because the time had gone by when they were to have been relieved, and nothing but rumours had yet arrived to encourage them. The most positive assurances of immediate relief were circulated. We were kept in a state of excitement by reports of distant guns, which seemed to come closer and closer, till many averred that they heard successive salvoes, and a straggling fire of musketry. For two nights, after Havelock had retired to Cawnpoor, our hopes of instant relief were sustained by a pony in a dark stable, whose tremulous efforts to shake off insects from his sides were echoed in a well close by!

Then a lull would come, which we employed in conjecturing the cause of our disappointment, and in endeavouring to persuade each other that myriads of troops were arriving in Calcutta, enraged by our wrongs and eager to avenge our dishonour. We drew lively pictures of long lines of infantry, artillery, and cavalry—veterans from the Crimea—advancing up the Grand Trunk Road, trampling out every vestige of rebellion, and, by their invincible courage, spreading consternation to the most distant spots. We used fancifully to march that prodigious army over India, stopping occasionally to annihilate contemptible hosts of rebels and mutineers, and to enforce a terrible retribution for the savage murder of the Innocents. We hung and slaughtered a fabulous number of "odious" creatures; for all were more and more convinced that mercy was misplaced, and that Asiatics could only be ruled in future by scorching rods of iron. Indeed, if a verdict of ours could have had effect, we would have left our defences, to wander down to the sea, through a wilderness of wreck and ruin. This heartless and ignorant temper will many years survive the extinction of the mutiny; and it is to be feared that it will still more estrange the people from their proud masters.

To a few, however, these lively visions of capering conquering armies afforded no solace. Fudge! they would pettishly say, all India is in arms to expel the hated foreigner, and that dangerously clever Emperor* will prevent the dispatch of an adequate number of troops. They would argue themselves into a vehement passion against the prevailing belief that England was pouring out her best troops to secure her great eastern gem, and appeal to our past experience as proof of their prognostic, that the extent of the disaster, and the necessity for immediate assistance, would be so slowly

* We should not deny to the Emperor Napoleon the debt due for his friendly forbearance during the war in India, because his present designs are inscrutable. He has hitherto done us no harm, and it is to be hoped that no policy of his will hereafter hurt our clever neighbours.

believed, that the empire could not be saved. The infatuation which blinded the officials in India, was, they urged, even greater in England, where old Indians abounded who would industriously deny the necessity, and accuse us of exaggerating the danger. Whilst we spoke, an army was landing which Providence had floated towards us, and we were saved.

These disappointments affected the minds of the natives, but especially the servants, who began to discredit the reports of spies and the letters, which Brigadier Inglis promptly circulated with the generous object of enlivening them. Desertions again occurred, which left some families without a single menial, and reduced the messes to great discomfort. The fear of the natives quitting us altogether occasioned anxiety, for their endurance of danger and privation with us was inexplicable: there was little reliance on their attachment, and small hope of their submitting to much more fatigue and starvation for our sakes. Brigadier Inglis, and his advisers, were conscious that our chief strength—and, indeed our salvation—lay in the retention of our Sepoys and followers; they, therefore, very discreetly encouraged them by paying liberally for extra labour, and by treating them with the kindness and consideration their valuable services merited. Their fidelity was one of those chances that enter into all the great contests of mankind, for which no cause is discoverable.

I was particularly fortunate in losing only one out of eleven servants, and Rujub Ali, (a Mahommedan to whom I had shown some kindness after the annexation of Oudh, by which he lost service,) voluntarily came in to me from the city on the second day of the siege; and, in this month, took out a despatch to Allahabad, which he safely delivered. He was promised a reward of money, and a situation for life, and I know not what else, for we were profuse in promises to induce men to undertake such hazardous tasks. He got only *twenty pounds*, and I had difficulty in getting a situation for him of two pounds a month; from which he was afterwards discharged. Captain Carnegie sent out two more of my servants with letters, one of whom was killed while leaving the entrenchment. The other was liberated by me from the Kaisur Bagh Palace, during the assault in March, 1858, and was afterwards shot by our own soldiers, in the streets of Lucknow, while making his way to my quarters. My cook, (good old Badoolla Khan!) had known me more than twenty years; and his wife, (who was wounded in the thigh by a bullet,) had nursed mine when an infant. These two old servants cheerfully did whatever was asked of them by any one, and the rest behaved well. It is impossible to overrate the assistance which these poor people were to me and my family in our extremity. Three of them were wounded.

I fast recovered my strength after August, and, when not on duty at my own post, was engaged shooting at the other garrisons. Man-shooting! as I then called it. The *Cawnpoor Battery* was a dangerous place, and an especial mark for the enemy's guns, which were about a hundred yards off. Colonel Palmer and myself one afternoon amused ourselves by firing at the gunners, and silenced them for some time, when we descended from the rampart to talk. I ascended again, and, as a sentry was warning me that the enemy had pointed one of their guns for the spot from whence I had teased them, an eighteen-pounder shot burnt my right ear and grazed my shoulder, drawing little blood, but greatly swelling and discolouring the skin. Myself and an artilleryman were violently thrown down, a sand bag having hit him on the chest. The enemy made repeated attempts to force this battery, but they were so spiritless, and had such an unconquerable dread of hand grenades, (which certainly are very dangerous), that they never got over our five-foot ditch. It was one of our worst built batteries, and the guns were withdrawn from it at the commencement of the defence.

I visited Mr. Gubbins's post occasionally, and observed him active with his rifle. The defences of his garrison were erected by himself, and he did some execution during the siege, for he was a good shot. It was the fashion to decry this gentleman before and during the siege, although he was one of the most active in preparing for it, and seemed to have a very correct notion of what would happen. He did as everybody else had the power of doing; but few had his forethought, and did not furnish their cellars. He has been accused of illiberality. When I was sick my wife troubled Mr. Gubbins for some soda-water: her request was twice complied with; and I saw that the sick and wounded were better served in his house than anywhere else. Although I think that he might have stinted himself and his friends a little more, it would be unjust to deny that he could have lived sumptuously but for his liberality to others. The clamour against him was not altogether fair, and it might have been more justly applied to others of the garrison, who gave *nothing* from their stores.

I visited all the posts, but most frequented one

known as *Innes's Garrison.** There were several civilians there, who, encouraged by their gallant young commander, Lieutenant Loughnan, had distinguished themselves in resisting the assaults, which were unusually vigorous at this weak point. It was almost the key of our position, but so little was this understood before the siege, that the Chief Engineer distinctly warned the civilians that it was needless entrenching themselves there, for it must be abandoned as untenable. Luckily, Mr. Parry (manager of the Delhi Bank), and his spirited son-in-law, Mr. Erith, (who was killed repelling one of the assaults,) continued the work, and this important post was saved. The house was reduced to ruins before the end of September, but the good spirits of the garrison never suffered in the least, and I spent some happy moments there. It was a dangerous post, for the enemy's sharp-shooters rarely missed an object, and none of them were ever tired of shooting. Captain Waterman, (who succeeded Lieut. Loughnan), was standing in the shade of a doorway with his glass, directing his riflemen, with little more than one hand exposed; he was observed, and soon sent running to the hospital with a broken thumb, pursued by me with a tumbler of spirits. Persons not liking to be shot, ran to and from the garrison through the fire of the enemy, as only frightened men can run; and on that occasion I just escaped by stumbling on my nose,

* One of the defences was known as the "Sago Garrison," because it had been used as a school house, prior to the siege, by Mrs. Elizabeth Sago. With the assistance of the king of Oudh, a school for the instruction of native female christians was established about twenty-five years ago by the Resident, General J. Low; and that amiable and most respectable widow lady undertook the arduous task of instructing them. She with difficulty survived the trials of the siege; lost all her property; and is now at South Warnbro, in Hants, endeavouring to live on the miserable pittance allowed by the Government of India, and the Relief Fund.

and crawling through the churchyard gateway. It was the first visit I made after leaving my bed, and my trembling legs were no match for Captain Waterman, who was quickly out of sight. Some of my war companions have asserted that I did not know what fear was, but if they had felt the palpitation of my heart, and seen me that day, they would have looked down upon as frightened a creature as ever licked the dust. I am not ashamed to confess that I was often affrighted afterwards, for there are certain helpless situations into which men are sometimes forced in war, by their own impetuosity, when they cannot help trembling, though they may conceal it.

Our famous Redan Battery was worth a visit; it was well raised and in a good commanding position. Our cannon and rifles often sent strings of people scrambling across the Iron Bridge spanning the river, to our extreme amusement: for there is nothing so droll as the external manifestations of fear. From it we commanded the opposite bank of the river, to which the enemy sometimes descended to bathe, and the women and children for water. Few of the former ventured within range, for, whether citizens or soldiers, they rarely escaped; but it soon became known that females and children might do so, as our gallant defenders never hurt them. I once heard men of the 32nd Foot object to shells which fell away from the mark, because they might hurt innocent women, and, on another occasion, condemn a comrade, who exclaimed aloud, that he would kill the "mother of a woman!"

The 32nd Foot behaved so admirably after the first month of the siege, that it would be ungenerous to complain of their proceedings at a time when all of us were more or less disorderly. We were particularly struck with their courageous bearing, and, indeed, reckless exposure of their lives; and the manner in which they endured privation, the most severe day and night duty, and constant exposure to sun and rain, almost without a murmur, could not have been exceeded by any troops in the world. Their officers were all worthy of their commissions. Brigadier Sir John Inglis, although excelled by some of the garrison, discharged his responsible and laborious duties with ability. He was always on the move, and most watchful, and never persisted in doing wrong when errors were respectfully explained to him. He is a good, plain honourable man, who deserved the distinction which Her Majesty has been pleased to confer for his indefatigable services during the memorable defence of Lucknow.

The enemy's efforts to force an entrance were neither many nor manful during the month of September, and nothing they could do then would have alarmed us, for we felt more than equal to them. Among the Europeans there was rather a liking for the hardy and hazardous life led for three months: for man was born for turmoil and trouble, and is sometimes glad to be rid of the restraints of civilization. War introduces queer fashions, and he was a proud man who could sport a red or green shirt, and a pair of rough inexpressibles, with the ends tucked into a pair of brown leather boots. One of our most amiable men,* (who died from the effects of the siege, after the relief,) bound up his legs with red tape,—by which, alas! our hands were often tied before;—and many carried,

* Lieutenant Hay, 48th Native Infantry.

absorbed in their clothes, the ink of the public offices, for that mixture bore much dirt without showing it.

The women, by this time, had resigned themselves to their fate, and the dear, kind, gentle creatures, were so patient, and so generous! Women shine brilliantly in all those qualities that are most needed in affliction. She bears travail and trouble heroicly, and is so unselfish. She welcomed her husband back from his dangerous duty with a sweet encouraging smile, for she would not damp his spirits! "There, dear soul! you must be so tired, and hungry, and I have cooked that horrid bit of beef so nicely for you," pointing to a savory morsel smoking under the greedy eyes of the hungry man. "But, dear wife, have you eaten any?"—Watch the affectionate flash of her beautiful eyes as she tells that heavenly falsehood! She sits by, gay and happy, while he devours his and her own share! I have several times known wives to hunger for the sake of their husbands and children, and I was told of one instance in which a husband starved himself, when food was scarce, to feed his wife and child. I am glad to record so noble an act of Mr. George Couper.

Towards the end of September we lost the most active and most daring man in the garrison, who, by his excessive zeal and intelligence, had enabled us to thwart almost every attempt of the enemy to destroy our defences by mining. Captain Fulton, of the Bengal Engineers, had the top of his head carried off by a round shot, when observing a battery of the mutineers. He was so conspicuously useful, and so indefatigable—whether sick or well—that he was known to all the defenders, who greatly deplored his death. He was kind and gentle, and did more, in his own quiet way, than anybody else. The Engineers were more or less remarkable for their ability and devotion during the siege, and their labours were of the utmost service. Fulton excelled them all. The Report of the Defence only says of this precious man, that he "afforded the most valuable aid," and "was indeed indefatigable."

CHAPTER VII.

Nature without and within—To the rescue—Casualties at the battle of Futteypoor—The enemy would let no one go near them—Cawnpoor—The valiant slow, and cowards fast runners—Bithoor twice occupied—A lucky return—Advance to Lucknow—City forced—Enemy drowned—The garrison saved by gallant soldiers—Dear Old England!—An impartial estimate of General Havelock's services—Brigadier Niell as good as him, and Sir James Outram better than either.

THE dark heavy clouds vanished which had shaded us from the fierce sun of September, and regularly poured down showers of rain to refresh us, and to revive all nature without, where the fields and groves were clothed in their rich autumnal vestments. Our longing and admiring eyes were often turned towards them: for nature is never so lovely as when the enjoyment of it is denied. The offensive odours which had sickened us for two months diminished under the influence of heat, while we grew weary of the dull monotony of our lives, and tired of watching for the relief promised by the beginning of August. The enemy remained sheltered in the buildings around us, awaiting the starvation of the garrison, depriving us of the little time left for repose by false attacks preceded by the noise of bugles and trumpets. Occasionally, we were enlivened by their musicians playing in the afternoon, *Marlbrook*,

Will you have me now? and such like airs, when drums and fifes would be added to the musical clatter, which always concluded with the National Anthem.

But relief was at hand. The army of the perfidious Nana of Bithoor had been impulsively carried off the proposed field of battle at Futteypoor: General Havelock's tired and hungry little force did all they could to catch them, after a march of twenty-four miles under a scorching sun. This spirited affair was accomplished without a casualty among the Europeans, excepting an officer of the 60th Rifles, who was overcome in an encounter with an ox, and a private of the 78th Highlanders, who intrepidly flew to the rescue, and got kicked for his trouble.

The indefatigable General, after a short rest, pursued the enemy up to the Pandoo Nuddee Bridge, where they only stayed to effect that most skilful manœuvre of getting away from a force that was thirsting for every drop of blood in their bodies. Here the casualities were twenty-five killed and wounded, and the enemy suffered little, as they engaged at a distance, and would let no one overtake them. But "the indomitable energy of the British troops rose superior to every trial,—instinct with the dignity of manhood, they uttered no complaint, but bore on nobly under the scorching sun, which glared down its unpitying rays upon their arms, which glittered with intolerable radiance, till the brain reeled and the eyeballs ached with the intensity of that dazzling sheen."*

The following day Cawnpoor was entered, and the enemy again skilfully manœuvred themselves out of the

* The "Journal of an English Officer in India," by Major North, of the 60th Rifles.

way, although those distinguished regiments, the 64th, the 78th, the 84th, and Rough Brayser's Sickhs, went in hot pursuit, and General Havelock himself led his successful flank movement, which is said to have completely surprised the mutineers. You will wonder, reader, that such surprising running should overtake no one, if you have never been in action and seen that troops go slower after danger than from it. There is this distinction, too, cowards are carried off the field, whereas the valiant have to carry themselves; which makes an important difference in the speed of each. For example, if you and I were to race for a wager from Temple Bar to that very remarkable National Gallery in Trafalgar Square that was built in the dark, perhaps you would win: but if you were to pursue me back, armed with an Enfield rifle and bayonet, I should undoubtedly recover the lost wager by a great many lengths.

The town of Bithoor was next entered, without a shot being fired, and then the devoted little force crossed into Oudh, where, notwithstanding that it encountered the most "obstinate resistance," and "suffered severely from a most withering fire,"* it lost only one hundred and forty men, many of whom where struck down by disease and exposure. The retrograde movement, afterwards made to Cawnpoor, cannot be overrated, for it assuredly saved that important position and preserved General Havelock's small army from destruction in the streets of Lucknow. Bithoor was once more entered; the troops this time encountering some opposition, in which they lost a few men

* The "Journal of an English Officer in India," by Major North, of the 60th Rifles.

killed and wounded, and had several disabled by the heat.

At Cawnpoor the fatigued and reduced force reposed till joined by fresh troops under General Sir James Outram, who chivalrously left it to General Havelock to relieve the garrison of Lucknow, (wrongly said to be in a deplorable state,) and attached himself to the volunteer cavalry. At Mungurwar the enemy were dislodged with a trifling loss to ourselves. Midway to Lucknow a royal salute was fired, but the garrison did not hear it. The Alum Bagh, on the verge of the city was reached, through a deluge of rain, after a little opposition; and during the halt the leaders were rejoiced by the sound of artillery, which gave them tidings of the existence of their suffering brethren.

On the morning of the 25th September, the final effort was made to reach the Residency, and in the afternoon we had the gratification of seeing our deliverers forcing their way to us in the direction of the Kaisur Bagh Palace. Our garrison was intensely eager to see even the smoke of that devoted band, and crowded to the roofs of the buildings, where they ardently listened to the booming artillery, and painfully strained their eyes for a sight of the contending troops. We turned occasionally to observe the streets of the city, which seemed to be agitated by the fears of the populace, and the preparations of the rebels, who ran from place to place, apparently appalled by the steady advance of our army. A peculiar buzz mingled with the incessant discharge of musketry and roar of artillery, upon the terrible effects of which we speculated with savage joy. At last the enemy came before us, retreating in the utmost disorder towards the bridge of boats, over the

Goömpty, which was beyond the range of our guns. Horses, camels, elephants, carts, carriages, and citizens and soldiers commingled, eagerly pressed on to the weak and narrow raft. Our troops seemed to be quickly pursuing, for the dense mass suddenly pressed forward—the bridge parted in the middle—the whole body violently struggled for awhile—and then went down! Oh! how exultingly we saw their despairing efforts, and watched for the avenging artillery. Several of the rebels and mutineers, divested of their arms, plunged into the rapid stream for safety, while thousands ran up and down the bank, making frantic gestures for boats from the opposite side. The cavalry leaped into the stream on their horses, who, in most instances dipped their riders off, and left them to perish, while they returned to shore to graze on the green grass close by.

We were disappointed! The host of fugitives, whom we would gladly have seen helplessly floating down the river, were needlessly alarmed. General Havelock's operations being necessarily confined to a narrow line, the panic on his right escaped observation, and he passed on to the RED GATE, through which it was his evil destiny to force his way. Up to this spot he had penetrated through the enemy at considerable sacrifice; but now the advance column had to run through a close rapid fire of small arms, which, in its effects, practically illustrated the selfish aphorism of *Every one for himself, and God for us all.* No one stopped to pick up the weary and the wounded, who were butchered by the mutineers as they closed in upon the rear. Over two hundred heads were afterwards paid for, and paraded by our dastasdly foe as trophies of victory!

The heroic little column was now in view. The anxious defenders of the Residency outpoured, in screams and gesticulations, their frenzy at the sight of the noble men, who dared do so much for their sakes, and for the glory of their country. From my elevated place on the roof of the Post Office, I cheered and waved my hat till tired, and sobbed as I rushed down to welcome our deliverers at the gateway. I ran from one to another, pressing the exhausted men and officers to drink my last three bottles of liquor; which they readily did, overpowering me with profuse thanks and blessings. Dear old England! you are just, generous, and mighty: it is an honour to be associated in your fame: may you always have such intrepid and enduring sons to confound your enemies!

General Havelock entered the Army in 1815. When war was declared against the Burmese, in 1825, he was appointed to the general staff of Sir Archibald Campbell, and published a simple history of the war. In 1838 he joined the Army of Cabool, as Aide-de-Camp to Sir Willoughby Cotton. In 1840 he published an account of this distant expedition, and, although his biographer states it will "long remain a lasting monument of the military science and brilliant genius of its author,"* the memoir has hitherto obtained little commendation, and does not seem to deserve such extravagant praise. He was in Jelalabad during the siege of 1842, and with Sir Hugh Gough, as Persian interpreter, throughout the Sickh campaign of 1846. Eleven years later he commanded a Brigade of the Persian expedition. General Havelock, up to that date, had served forty-three years without attaining a greater reputation than his con-

* "Biographical Sketch of Sir Henry Lawrence," by the Rev. Wm. Brock.

temporaries. Indeed, he had no opportunity of displaying his military talents. and it is doubtful whether they were so great as the public in their haste, and his friends in their generous zeal, have since attributed to him. He had always been known as an earnest student of his profession, as a chivalrous soldier, and as a man of the highest integrity, who did not fear to avow his religious convictions.

The advance for the relief of Cawnpoor and Lucknow was only remarkable for the dastardly conduct of the enemy, and for the patience and spirit with which General Havelock, and his small army, endured fatigue and exposure at a season of the year when the weather is most trying to the European constitution. It is perfectly absurd to mention the engagements of Havelock, up to the Alum Bagh, as *pitched battles*, for the enemy invariably broke ground the moment he seriously threatened them; and, that the fighting was not sanguinary, may be inferred from the very small number of men killed and disabled on either side. With a despicable foe there was no need of great skill, nor was much applied to vanquish the disorganized rebels and mutineers, who invariably vanished of their own accord when encountered on the plains.

The passage through the city to the beleagured garrison of Lucknow was as daring and as hazardous an enterprize as could have been attempted, but much of the credit of its success is due to the subordinate officer and to the common soldier, for it was accomplished by indomitable courage alone. It is far from my wish to detract from the merit of so good an officer as the late Sir Henry Havelock; but I, for one, respectfully venture to pronounce against ranking him with the

Great Commanders of England. If so little will place a man there AT ANY OTHER TIME, there will be no knowing, by-and-bye, which are the illustrious Chiefs of the country. Had the late Brigadier Niell commanded the force, he would have accomplished as much. His death in the Red Gate was sincerely deplored by the troops, who esteemed him highly, for he had shown ability, courage, and decision, of a kind that eminently fitted him for the hard emergency of the time.

The public were ungenerous to one, who, more than any other General, merited their applause. The fame of the man of many deeds, who, for his manly and chivalrous bearing, had years ago been styled the Bayard of the Indian Army, was forgotten when England was convulsed with joy at the success of Havelock's exaggerated battles. The greatest achievement was the reinforcement of the garrison of Lucknow, and Sir James Outram was the most forward man in accomplishing it. With rare generosity he accorded the honour to another.

CHAPTER VIII.

Guide Havelock's heavy guns and wounded—A shameful failure—Nine heroes—First sortie, and a hasty return home—A brave Pandee rewarded—Sepoys behaved well with us, and mutineers would have done better with good leaders—Second sortie more successful—Feeble attempt to open a road to Alum Bagh—Captain Wade—Pickles and preserves the death of Major Haliburton—A house taken, retaken, and not taken—Alum Bagh project abandoned—Volunteer Engineers—First crawl through the mines—First encounter in the bowels of the earth, a Sepoy wounded—Second Adventure, two mortally wounded—Brasyer a good soldier—Siekhs ought to be brought to England and exhibited: an idea for the wise.

THE time had now come when I could be of more service than was previously practicable, and I eagerly seized every chance of being useful to the force. With Sir James Outram came my early friend Colonel Robert Napier, who readily availed himself of my service in making his arrangements for the passage of the heavy artillery, and wounded, through the Chutter Munzil Palace; which was effected by a road screened from the view of the enemy nearly the whole distance. We had but two men wounded in an operation that would have been impossible in the direction followed by Generals Outram and Havelock.

The heavy guns having to pass under a close fire from the Red Gate, I offered to guide a party, after dark, to take it by surprise, and Colonel Napier entrusted the attack to me. I led it into the square before the gate, (where lay our wounded in the doolies dropped the previous evening), without alarming the enemy, who could be distinctly heard overhead, and behind a screen drawn across the passage. In three minutes the Gate would have been ours, but, at the moment for action, the two young officers in command urged that the enemy were too many, and being overheard by the men, they at once whispered their concurrence, and alluded to me as a drunken madman. I did reel, indeed, from the effects of pain and fatigue; I was many hours on my feet, and my toes had been severely squeezed by Captain Hardinge's horse. In vain I urged the certainty of success, and the necessity for holding the gate while our heavy guns passed by: my party retired, pursued by a sharp fire from the enemy, who were warned by their noisy flight. We had unconsciously been close to nine devoted men, who, shut up in a house for two nights and a day, had resisted the persevering efforts of the enemy to destroy them, and endeavoured to preserve the wounded in the doolies—the victims of General Havelock's too great haste to reach the Residency.

Dr. Home, in his very interesting account of that gallant defence, thus alludes to our failure:—"About two a.m. we heard a heavy firing close to us, and a great rush of the enemy over our heads. We now felt certain that our situation was known, and that the firing proceeded from a party sent to our relief. To describe the revulsion of feeling is impossible. We raised a cry of Europeans! Europeans! and then united to give one loud cheer, and shouted with all our might Charge them! charge them! keep on your right!" The shout was addressed to men who heard nothing besides the fire of the enemy, which the Doctor and his exhausted companions mistook for ours.

In the afternoon of the 27th September a sortie was led, by Major Stephenson of the Madras Fusileers, into a battery on the left of the Cawnpoor Road, and I accompanied it as a volunteer. We captured and spiked three guns after much firing, when, from want of confidence in the guide, and uncertainty as to where we were, the commander became confused—our men grew uneasy standing still—the enemy crowded forward, encouraged by yells and bugles—and we scrambled out of the battery, and followed our inclinations home. Although misadventures will happen with the best of troops, I was rather disappointed at the two samples witnessed within a few hours, and began to think that we should never get out of our poor old defences. As we lingered in the battery a Sepoy of the 13th Native Infantry, who came out as a pioneer, advanced to a broad opening through which the enemy kept up a brisk fire, and, flourishing his pick-axe, called to the Europeans to follow him to another gun, till he was shot down. But the uproar and confusion at that moment was such that nobody heeded him, and he would have been left behind had I not helped him out of the battery, and put him on the road, along which I was myself in full flight soon after. The gallantry of this fine Pandee was reported; Sir James Outram raised him to the rank of an officer, and gave him the Order of Merit; and he died. Several Sepoys were conspicuous during the siege for gallantry, and their patient endurance of fatigue and privation was not excelled by ourselves: their fidelity, indeed, saved us. Foreigners had better not judge of the capabilities of the Sepoy from the ease with which the European defeated him; for timid leaders diminish, if they do not wholly extinguish, courage in their followers.

On the morning of the 2nd October the same batteries were attacked by a stronger detachment of troops, under the orders of Colonel Robert Napier. I attached myself to the party with Captain Shute, of the 64th Foot; which forced its way over a stockade into the enemy's battery amidst a terrific rattle of musketry, loud calls to COME, and fierce orders from the rear to GO. The troops ran to the large house in the centre of the garden, from the top of which they looked for the enemy. I took a direction to the left, and at once learnt the whereabouts of the guns, (which the enemy had withdrawn,) by two shots passing in quick succession through the wall I had mounted, carrying the bricks thick among the dozen soldiers and civilians who followed me. I stayed for a couple of minutes studying the ground, exposed to a misdirected fire of muskets, then brought down Captain Shute from the roof of the house, and led him unobserved upon the left flank of the mutineers, which compelled them to abandon their first gun. Here we remained, sheltered behind the wings of a gateway, making a prodigious noise about the one we had got, while the enemy harmlessly poured grape from a second gun, till Captain Shute and Lieutenant Brown rushed through the opening, and quite frightened them away from it, and from a very little gun at the top of a street. Owing to the flank movement, which surprised the enemy, and to their rank cowardice, we did not lose a single man in securing the three guns.

The guns were burst—a few traders were killed,

including a very aged man, hiding under the petticoat of his venerable wife, for whom I pleaded in vain to men who laconically uttered the favourite war-whoop CAWNPOOR!—the garden house was blown down—the shops in the neighbourhood were pillaged—and I carried screaming to my quarters an old cock, a bosom full of sour oranges, and a heart filled with pride for the share I had had in that day's glory.

The following morning Colonel Napier sent me to Major Haliburton of the 78th Highlanders, who had orders to open a communication, straight through the city, to the garrison at the Alum Bagh. The advance was led by Captain Wade of the 90th Foot, who marched nearly half a mile to the mansion of Nawab Moontaz-ood-doolah, where he was stopped by a fierce fire of matchlocks from a handsome mosque close by. As neither the strength nor position of the enemy could be satisfactorily ascertained from the mansion, I attempted to discover both by crossing the street further up, exposed to a severe fire, which drew them from under cover towards me. Captain Wade, who never is to be outdone in spirit, ran over through a severer fire, and after surveying them as long as he prudently could, we scampered back, pursued by numerous bullets and cries of Maro! Maro! from fellows who made a feint of following us. Captain Wade made indifferent use of his very long legs, and I nearly butted him through the wicket in my anxiety to escape.

Major Haliburton, who had unavoidably been detained, now joined the party, and requested I would return with him to explain to Sir James Outram the position we had reached; but unfortunately for that kind-hearted and gallant officer a room was discovered in the Nawab's mansion stored with pickles and preserves. I filled my coat pockets with sugar, and secured a jar of preserves under each arm, and a third in my hand, to take to my family, when Major Haliburton, who had incautionsly gone to the door facing the mosque, fell mortally wounded while calling his men away from those "damned jams and gingers!" some of which he was eating. He died next day, to the great grief of his fine regiment.

According to his request, I returned without delay to Sir James Outram, unincumbered by the preserves, which the gallant men of the Fusileers devoured whilst I was attending to their wounded leader. Colonel Napier brought me back, but in the meantime an order had reached the detachment to retire, and another party was taken on, under the command of Major Stephenson of the Madras Fusileers, which re-occupied the empty mansion, and was greeted in the upper rooms with a fire from the mosque that drove it into the back apartments. Here Colonel Napier and Major Stephenson were standing behind a thick door questioning me, when a bullet passed through the panel and struck the latter officer, who died several days later. The mansion was again abandoned during the night, and barricaded by the enemy, who repulsed an assault made in the morning to recover it. Street fighting needed rapidity of movement; for, in such attacks, hesitation strenghtened, and promptitude weakened, an enemy who would not wait to be cut off from the means of escape.

The project of reaching the Alum Bagh was abandoned, for there was nothing so good as staying as we were, giving employment to a host of enemies, who, had we retired, would have been free to threaten our communication with the sources from whence we were gathering strength at Cawnpoor. Attention was now turned to improving old defences, and constructing new ones for the relieving force located in the palaces. Three sides of the Residency had been cleared of the enemy's guns; officers and volunteers were temporarily appointed to the Engineers to superintend the defences, and Europeans and natives were enrolled as miners. Colonel Napier procured my appointment as an Assistant Field Engineer, and I set to work to maintain the character for zeal and courage that, to my great joy, I had already won with the assistance of my generous comrades. Our operations were small at first; but the activity of the enemy, who sprang some mines that did us damage, soon obliged the Engineers to begin making extensive defensive, or listening galleries, to protect the advanced posts, which were so close to the enemy that we might have spat in their faces.

The first attempt to blow up the enemy recoiled on ourselves, and an excellent miner of the 32nd Foot, and myself, were nearly buried in the ruins of our own building, as the Chief Engineer watched for the effects in the opposite direction! This was the virgin mine of one of the most active and intelligent Engineers in the service; and its failure goes to prove what I have said before, that men who have never been in war know little of its wants. Perhaps, had the thing been left to myself, the whole force of the powder would have come up the shaft before me, notwithstanding the haste with which I left it; and you would never have heard of "Lucknow Kavanagh."

What a nervous moment was that first crawl on all-fours through a long, narrow, cold, damp mine, appalled by the darkness, and a fancy that an enemy may have got in wishing to blow out my shrinking brains, or that it might fall in and bury me alive! It tried me considerably, and I had to say a great many encouraging things to myself to calm my agitated heart, which vehemently panted for the light again. Indeed, it cost many efforts to appease my fears, and gain confidence in those subterranean ramifications, in which I sometimes strayed, at night, despairing of ever getting out. At last I discovered that a resolute man was more dangerous below than above ground, and I soon had an opportunity of testing my spirit in the bowels of the earth.

The enemy were heard mining in the south corner of the Siekh quarters, and the Engineers countermined to stop them; but they had done so much before being discovered, that we broke in about three feet from our own shaft, and the miners escaped. At this moment I relieved the officer on duty, and went down with a revolver, conjecturing that the enemy would send in some one to see what had disturbed the miners. After waiting awhile a Sepoy descended with his musket, and advanced to my end of the gallery, where it was quite dark, whereas the light streamed down at his. I let him come in about his own length, and then shot him through the shoulder. I pursued him, and fired again, but the cap snapped, and he escaped, roaring with pain. The enemy let water into the gallery, and an hour after it fell in.

Another day, while crawling through the galleries, I heard their miners at work, and for two hours I sat watching for them as they noiselessly approached. A small hole was first made, through which the miner thrust the handle of his tool to try what it led to, for they knew nothing of our listening galleries; as he withdrew it, I shoved down the narrow partition with my hands, and put a pistol to his breast. It missed fire again and again as I went in after him, and he scrambled out screeching with fear. I waited in the gallery, thinking it probable that one of the Sepoys would venture in; and, after much squabbling as to who should do it, a Sepoy jumped down, cautiously keeping his body back from the mouth of the gallery. He put his musket in towards me, showing no more than his hand; I felt certain that he would look before he fired, and reserved my shot. It was a hazardous moment, for whichever fired first was sure to hit. Fortune favoured me! As he stooped, his left arm and shoulder was exposed—my bullet passed through it—and he lost no time in getting out to his comrades.

The miner in his haste dropped his tools in the shaft, and the mutineers (who were only about three yards from me) threatened to shoot him if he did not fetch them. The poor creature remonstrated most sorrowfully, and my heart sickened as he prayed, before descending, that they would see to the support of his family. He leaped down crying "Mercy! mercy!" I could not fire a second time, as he slowly climbed out wounded, exclaiming he was dead! I grieved that our own imminent danger made it compulsory to intimidate the enemy's miners, so as to render it difficult to obtain the services of such men.

My duty was at the mosque, and at the quarters of the Ferozepoor regiment of the Siekhs, who came in with General Havelock, under the command of Major Brasyer: a soldier who, fourteen years ago, was promoted from the ranks for conspicuous gallantry in the Sutledge campaign of Lord Gough, and has since so much improved his good reputation, that his name is now familiar to most persons conversant with the history of the mutiny. He looks like a Siekh, and is as rough as any one of them. I was never associated with better soldiers than these, and, like many more of the same singular nation, they often led us to victory during that unnatural war. They never shrink from danger that is faced by their officers, and are more disposed to fraternize with Europeans than any other Asiatic of caste.

Why not show some of these warriors to the people of Europe, where I believe, there would be little difficulty in persuading them to go? They are sociable and intelligent; and, if relieved after a term, they would—if the Siekhs returned at all—carry back habits and sentiments that would be of the utmost use in introducing the civilized ideas of the West. The instruction of the people of India can only be effected through themselves, and nothing will enlighten them so much as ocular evidence of the prosperity and superiority of Europeans at home. Could they be socially mixed up with us, those prejudices which seem to be indestructible would fade away in the new light. I throw out this "idea" in the hope that some one may catch it who can give it a tangible form. There are duties in England which could be discharged by Siekhs, who are very apt at learning English.

CHAPTER IX.

Champions of the people—A promise to go down to the sea more than fulfilled—The warriors of Oudh see the defences and blow alarming sounds—A Council wants two hundred thousand pounds, and cannot get it—A crockery room and British bayonets—Colonel Purnell—Havelock's troops, trumps, and smokers—Captain Crommelin—Sir Robert Napier—A great adventure in the mines, two men shot—Familiar talk with the enemy—Greased cartridges provoked a mutiny—Lieutenant Grant—Somebody to be hung—Good news.

I OUGHT to have mentioned before that the fifteen or twenty thousand rebels and mutineers who were scared away by the arrival of reinforcements, returned to the city, accompanied by many more attracted by the prowess of the hundred thousand armed beings who plundered the weak and simple, and strutted through the city with all the confidence and none of the virtues of champions of the people. These simple folks were clean gone at the delicious prospect before them of cutting us up to a man; of establishing a most perfect government of disorder, to let every one earn a livelihood in any way he liked, limited only by the strength of the passions which God had given him; and at the promise of their chiefs to lead them down to the sea: which has been more than fulfilled in the case of some, who have actually crossed over to the penal settlement on the Andamans!

The city swarmed with the warriors of Oudh, and of

course we had to look sharp after ourselves, for they often came so near as to see our defences, when shot and shell flew about in a style which it was pleasant to look on, for they scarcely hit anyone. The reckless men would sometimes work themselves up to such a frenzy as to impiously shoot at the sky, when no amount of inaction could force them to leave the shelter of their defences, albeit that the Residency was encircled by brazen instruments of war blowing out the most alarming sounds, which meant they were to assemble and advance. But it happened sometimes that a "Council" would sit twelve hundred yards from us, and decide that the reduced finances of the state made it indispensable that the two hundred thousand pounds unlawfully retained by the obstinate Europeans should be theirs. The rabble would then approach imprudently close, with their officers grouped round the standards in the rear, to retire with the dead and dying the moment they saw that we were resolved not to let them have it.

On one occasion, indeed, their zeal took them far into a room of the palace, strewed a foot deep with broken crockery, when there was the most dreadful clatter of plates and clamour of angry and despairing voices, as our troops, recovering from their surprise, met them with fixed bayonets; which, to judge from the execution done that day by the 90th Foot, are the most awful things in the world in British hands. I humbly assisted on the occasion to disturb the calm deliberations of the enemy, by following along the roofs of the houses and dropping hand grenades among them, so that the warriors were greatly puzzled where to go, despite of a violent inclination to go somewhere. Colonel Purnell, who commanded in the palace, by his judicious arrangements and constant watchfulness, put it quite out of the power of the enemy to get so far again, supposing there was any disposition to go into a place from whence no one had ever returned. We were greatly pleased with this officer's cool courage, and the calm gentlemanly manner in which he gave directions and then saw them executed. I was often with H.M. 90th Foot, and I have reason to remember them all with pride and pleasure.

The troops that came in with General Havelock brought no more than the clothes on their backs, and no liquor was issued to them; but they shifted for themselves, quite as well as any Frenchman would have done, and cared nothing for danger, or exposure, or anything else, so long as they had a pipe of dry tea, or bitter leaves, or tobacco, to envelope their heads in smoke. These fine fellows were a terror to the enemy, and from the fact of their being tattooed, were considered to be soldiers especially selected from the flower of our army.

Our chief engineer, Captain Crommelin, was confined to his room with a very sore foot, and, as he is one of those active men who are everywhere at the same time, and have a provoking habit of harrying sluggards, some of us were not sorry for it. But there was another of those tiresome officers who never would lie down, and kept his and our legs perpetually on the move, giving quite as much employment to our eyes; for, if once lost, we had again to go over every step of the ground to find him. He poked his nose into queer places, and, whilst we stood shivering near him, would stare straight in the faces of the enemy, as if powder and shot were nonexistents. Colonel Robert Napier was, in fact, a most dangerous man to be with; for if you escaped being shot by the enemy, you only lived to be walked to death. This is an officer who hates figures, but has the strongest liking for facts. He is without the least fear, and, when his mind is made up, he follows it quickly. He is one of the most intelligent officers in the service, and his good sense is proverbial. His private virtues are those of every good man, and I have the best reason to say so. Had our gracious Queen knighted myself, I could not have been better pleased than when I saw this good, kind friend, dubbed for his meritorious services during the war. It is the prayer of many that he may survive to win more laurels in China, where he has gone to bring that vain and provoking nation to its senses.

Examining the new and visiting the finished mines was very dirty work, and my wardrobe was too poor for many changes. I brought away some coarse canvas from the deserted stores of the palace; and, with the assistance of a charming little lady, (who showed me how to cut them), I peeled the skin off my fingers sewing a tunic and overalls: the women laughing at my awkward first essay at tailoring. Sir Robert Napier once said that I would quickly learn anything, and sure enough, in a couple of days I met the admiring gaze of my comrades in a very business-like suit, and henceforth crept through the galleries dry and warm, and altogether very much at home.

The dress was new on my back, and the conceit of it not yet gone out of my silly head, when the enemy must needs make another and last attempt to blow us up in the vicinity of the Siekhs, who complimented me by naming me the *Burra Surungwalla*, or Great Miner, and now anxiously waited for the result, as I entered the mine and sat, like a cat patiently waiting for her prey. Slowly and cautiously the enemy's miner lessened the partition of earth between us, and, in two hours, a too heavy stroke of his placed us face to face. His eyes glared with fear as he spread out his arms screaming, and fell back mortally wounded into the shaft, where he lay moaning pitifully. The gallery was unusually large, but not more than six or eight feet from the pit, we being separated from the enemy, at the Siekh quarters, only by a few yards. I widened the opening, and crawled in to get to the mining tools, but they were too far, and I lay still, wondering what would come of the great noise at the top of the mine. They loudly called to each other to go down and fetch the dying miner and his implements, amidst the jingle of ramrods, an unusual uproar, and fierce resolves not to be outdone this time. I began to think I had ventured too near, and was speculating upon the probability of the pistol missing fire, when down came a Sepoy to solve the question by receiving a bullet in his stomach, before he could discharge his musket. I had forgotten to load my revolver, and was now left with only one shot more, which I reserved.

The commotion above grew louder and louder, and the fellows blustered and swore as if the whole body of them were coming down to me. I was close enough to see their feet by placing my face to the floor of the mine, and I now taunted them with cowardice in the profane language that is so often, and so well spoken by Englishmen to their followers, and so raised their ire that one swaggered and swore, in a superior style, that he'd go and kill me. I laughed and tried to provoke them to come in, till they thought of firing into the mine, and drove me back to my own gallery, nearly suffocated with smoke and blinded from earth the bullets threw up; which gave them an opportunity of hooking up the two wounded men who were groaning their lives out.

I returned to the same spot after a few minutes, protected by a couple of Siekhs, (who watched from our gallery), and then we commenced a very pleasant and harmless abuse of each other. I was upbraided for associating with cursed *Feringies*, who ate cow's meat, and did other abominations; which convulsed the Siekhs with laughter, for they perceived that I was mistaken for one of them, to whom such things are horrible. I told them at once that it was a European officer who spoke, when, to my surprise, the noise ceased. They civilly listened as I reproached them with ingratitude—condemned their infamous conduct to helpless women and children—their pusillanimity when confronted by us—and presented to them a picture of the ruin in which themselves and their families were sure to be soon involved.

"Why," I asked, "have you mutined, and what can you expect from the atrocities you have perpetrated?"

"We are fighting for our religion, which you meant to destroy."

"In what manner have we threatened your faith?"

"By giving us GREASED CARTRIDGES," was the prompt response.

"That was a mistake," I answered, "which the Government took the utmost pains to explain, and you were earnestly, and truly assured, that it had no intention of disregarding your religious prejudices. Did you ever know the British Government to make false professions? Has it not always spoken the truth?"

There was perfect silence for awhile, when a voice, as if affected by the truth, remarked, "It is true!" Then there was quietness again, as if all were thinking. But, if they thought at all, their reveries were immediately disturbed by a command, in an authoritative voice, to fire, which they did so carelessly that there was no need this time to shift backwards. I mocked them, and challenged the officer to come down and fetch the tools, to which he replied that he had plenty, and would give me some if I came for them. The Sepoys were once more desired to fire at me, and refused, urging that they "wished to hear the Sahib speak!" I caused them to laugh at the officer, by asking him to wait till I fetched some women's apparel, and kept them in humour with a fanciful account of our inexhaustible supplies—the speedy approach of the army which I have once before described as overrunning India—and endeavoured in vain to draw information from them.

They began filling up the mine with earth, but stopped whenever I spoke, sometimes calling to me to go on. I felt a foolish pride to possess the implements which lay nearly in the shaft, or pit, and told the Sepoys, at the opening of our conversation, that I would have them, and was answered by a defiance, for they were right under their guns. When I thought my talk had diverted their attention, I brought away the tools by a sudden spring, which so alarmed them, that only two men stayed to fire, and they were in such trepidation that both missed me at a distance of five or six feet. "Well done!" exclaimed the Siekhs and Sepoys in concert, as I retreated to my own gallery to watch the closing of the pit, which was now set about in earnest. In an hour more the adventure was over, and I went home to tell what I had done, very much pleased with myself and with everybody else in the world—which isn't a bad one.

On another occasion, and in another direction of the defences, I sat *nine hours* in a mine waiting for the enemy to come in; but they worked so slowly that about three feet of the distance remained when I quitted the spot at 7 o'clock P.M., wet, cramped, and hungry. We knew, from the direction, that the enemy's gallery was a long one, and I was in hopes that it would give me a chance of bringing in alive the miner or miners for Sir James Outram and his able Chief of the Staff. About 12 o'clock at night Lieutenant Innes broke in, but the miners being warned by some one coughing, they put out the light and escaped.

Lieutenant Grant, of the Madras Fusileers, who commanded at this place, was wounded through the stomach soon after, and we were deprived of the services of a very active, judicious, and gallant officer, who, strange to say, has recovered from the effects of the wound, and is doing duty with his regiment, if the astounding courage of Earl Canning has not forced it out the service.

It is vain to say, but it may be of use to me for the reader to know, that I was the only officer during the siege, who had any successful subterranean encounters with the enemy, because it always happened that I was on duty when they came. My comrades were up to such hazardous work, and there were few who would not have done it as well, if not better than myself.

Our chivalrous General, Sir James, used jokingly to surprise his visitors who were not in the secret, by saying, that, as the articles of war condemned a man to death for conferring with an enemy, Kavanagh was to be hung! When I was a wild lad, ready for any mischief, my uncle used to say that such was the fate that awaited me.

After October the old and new garrisons were in high spirits, for tidings reached us of the preparations for our rescue, and we already sniffed, in imagination, the savory viands and inspiring draughts, long absent from our covetous eyes. The few numbers of the *Home News*, and fragments of Indian papers brought in by Havelock's force, were eagerly perused by us over and over again, and it was soothing to our outraged feelings to learn from them that all England was affected for us, and that the intrepid little army which had manfully resisted the enemy against great odds, had eventually been rewarded by the complete capture of Delhi.

I have now come down to the time when I went out to bring in Sir Colin Campbell to the relief of my suffering brothers and sisters, and, the story being a long one, I shall go over to another chapter, where I hope you will do me the honour of following me, for it is one of the recompenses I desire for doing my duty.

CHAPTER X.

Mutiny remarkable for deeds of individual daring—A spy from Sir Colin Campbell—Arguments for despatching a European to guide the relieving force—A struggle for life—Proposal to Colonel Napier—Sir James Outram's reasons for consenting—A painful parting, and an affectionate heart—Disguise—Denied by Friends—A black painting, by General Outram—A brave parting—Captain Hardinge—YOU WILL NEVER BE FORGOTTEN.

ALTHOUGH my place in the garrison was very humble, the measures necessary for its defence, and for our succour, gave me as much concern as anybody in it. I was constantly reviewing in my mind the circumstances of our position in Lucknow, and imagining the probable state elsewhere. Mine is a temper that is little disturbed by the ordinary affairs of life, and my best energies were evoked by the amazing events of the time. It was a period when the power and glory of England were maintained by individual exertion more than by a combination of strength, and it will, hereafter, be proudly pointed to as affording the most remarkable evidence of the zeal and devotion of Britons when separately tried. The record of the mutiny is replete with examples of heroism, and, when the New Zealander surveys the ruins of London, he will wonder that such a fate should have overtaken so great a nation, if the events of this year, with all its wailing and clangor, pass through his thoughts. The battles of India will bear no comparison with the great contests in which the follies and passions of men have, to the latest period, involved the fairest countries of the world, and the ablest of mankind; but for those deeds of courage and self-devotion which have exalted England among nations, nothing so grand as the story of the mutiny will be found in her history.

On the morning of the 9th of November, 1857, I was apprised of the arrival of a spy, who effected an entry during the night, with a despatch conveying intelligence of a force coming from Cawnpoor. I had some days previously witnessed the drawing of plans by my young friend, Mr. James May, which were prepared, by direction of Sir James Outram, to assist the Commander-in-Chief in his advance upon the Residency. It then occurred to me that some one of intelligence, with the requisite local knowledge, ought to attempt to reach His Excellency's force beyond, or at the Alum Bagh, because the plans would be of little use without some one to explain them. The arrival of Sir Henry Havelock on the 25th of September might have been the destruction of the besieged, for he forced his way, believing that our supplies were nearly exhausted, and was himself enclosed! It was a grave fault, a very grave fault, misleading that officer as to the extent of our supplies, and Havelock is not to blame for his impetuous and chivalrous zeal to reach us. But the loss of life that day might have been far greater, and the result even less favourable, were it not for the presence of the Volunteer General, who did know something of the city, though little of the position of the enemy.

The enemy were stronger in November, and it was to be expected that the obstacles, along the route to be forced by Sir Colin Campbell, would be greater now than when General Havelock passed. I learnt from the spy that His Excellency's force was not large, and conjectured that the caution which that would oblige, combined with imperfect information, might delay the relief, which the movements of the Gwalior troops rendered urgent. If they succeeded in surrounding the little entrenchment at Cawnpoor, or, if his communication over the river Ganges, were imperilled before we could be rescued, what was the Commander-in-Chief to do? Our supplies were nearly exhausted; our sick and wounded were perishing for the want of absolute necessaries; and every day added to our calamities and endangered our position. One failure anywhere would have destroyed us, we were so greatly outnumbered. It was not improbable that a leader might suddenly be found, with the required spirit and influence, to conduct the rebels and mutineers to victory: for the valour of the defenders was not so great a security as the cowardice of the besiegers. The history of wars and revolutions show how capricious is fate in the production of successful chiefs; how they may suddenly emerge from a shrinking people to infuse courage, and lead them to victory. Sir James Outram had certainly furnished the Commander-in-Chief with plans and specifications, which had been devised with much care; but they were *for a certain route.* Circumstances might render that route impracticable—a contingency of war, common enough in the open field, and much more likely to occur in an immense city; or a better route might be unexpectedly opened to him by the folly of the enemy, which Sir Colin might not be able to use for the want of accurate information as to the nature of the ground, and the position of the enemy with reference to it.

Full and precise information is at all times valuable, but when every moment's hesitation costs a life it is priceless. The chances and accidents of war no general can always foresee, and he who engages an enemy, ignorant of his whereabouts and of their resources, is sure to be embarrassed if compelled to alter his plan of attack.

Swayed by these facts and reflections, I imparted to the spy, Kunoujee Lal, (who before the outbreak, had been a Nazir, or Bailiff, in one of our courts in Oudh), my desire to venture in disguise to the Alum Bagh, where he was to return in the night with a despatch for Sir Colin Campbell. I had not seen him before, but his shrewd intelligence and previous good service as a spy, at once secured my confidence. He made no attempt to frighten me by exaggerating the dangers of the road, but at first positively declined to incur the additional risk to which the company of a second person, and he a European, was sure to expose him. A couple of hours afterwards I persuaded Kunoujee Lal to run that danger, by holding out to him the prospect of an unusually good reward, and explaining to him the great public service he would thereby render to the British garrison. He then strongly urged that we should leave the defences by different roads, and meet outside the city; but he gave it up on learning that I knew too little of the intricacies of the city to venture alone, and on hearing a specimen of my Hindoostanee, which, though good, might not have stood the test of a too long examination under the crushing sensations of death.

I now sought a lonely spot where I could commune with myself, for until I secured a proper companion I would not prepare myself for the worst. I sat amazed at my boldness, unable to concentrate my thoughts, which came and went with a vehemence I had never felt before. Gradually, as the awfulness of death crept into my bewildered mind, the perturbation extended to the heart, and it beat violently against my side. The feelings of both overpowered me, and came pouring out in large drops through my eyes, as I sat with a flushed face buried in my hands. This precious effort of nature relieved me, but the attempts made, over and over again, to think calmly of the enterprize, only brought back the agitation; and I was obliged, at last, to seek the company of my comrades to compose myself. Whilst conversing with those fine fellows, I deliberated in my mind, and by two o'clock in the afternoon, resolved to volunteer my services through Colonel Robert Napier. I was impelled to the step I now took only by a sense of DUTY.

Colonel Napier expressed surprise at the offer, and at once pronounced the attempt impracticable, his features relaxing into a smile as he said so, for he evidently regarded the proposal as most absurd. He was, however, so much pleased with this further evidence of the zeal of his *protégé*, that he went into the Chief Commissioner to mention it, followed by me. Sir James Outram listened as I disclosed the reasons for wishing to go out, and figuratively placed them in one hand, and my life in the other, and asked whether the advantages were not weighty enough to overbalance his scruple to adventure a single life. He was not less astonished than Colonel Napier; but, in the true spirit of chivalry, he at once conceived and appreciated the motives of my proposition, and reasoned with me upon the probability of success. He frankly confessed that he thought it of the utmost importance that a European officer, acquainted with the localities and buildings intervening between the Dilkooshah and the Residency, should be provided to guide the relieving force, should its commander determine on advancing by that route; but that the impossibility of any European being able to escape through the city undetected, deterred him from ordering any officer to go, or even seeking volunteers for such a duty. He observed that my services as a guide would be very valuable, and that he, therefore, with difficulty resisted the temptation to accept my disinterested offer, of which he thought he ought not to avail himself. I was, however, so earnest in my entreaties to be allowed to go, that he yielded, provided he was satisfied with the disguise, and that I was of the same mind when the hour for departure arrived. After Sir James had explained to me his plans and the course which he advised Sir Colin Campbell to follow, he pressed me not to hesitate abandoning the adventure, if I wished to do so on further consideration. It was fortunate that such an officer as Sir James Outram was in command, as it required a man of more than ordinary capacity to understand and appreciate my motives, and to consent to so hazardous an enterprize. The friends of that able officer will understand how his chivalrous and generous heart suffered while doubtful of the fate of "the Guide," who deemed it no small honour to be engaged in executing his plan for the relief of the Lucknow garrison.

I was satisfied that the matter had so far progressed

well. I had secured an active guide—had made up my mind to die—and obtained the sanction of the General to go. The most difficult task that remained was to part from those who were most dear to me in the world! I lay down on the bed with my back towards my wife, who was giving her children the poor dinner to which they were now reduced, and endeavouring to silence their repeated requests for more. I dared not face her; for her keen eye and fond heart would have immediately detected that I was in deep thought, and agitated. She called me to partake of a coarse cake, but, as I could no more have eaten it than have eaten herself, I pleaded fatigue and sleepiness, and begged to be let alone. Of all the trials I ever endured this was the worst! The most kind and affectionate of women had been my companion for nearly thirteen years, through which she had patiently and courageously endured much trouble and discomfort for my sake. We were happy and contented to go on together the whole tenure of our lives surrounded by our family. The efforts I made to suppress all outward manifestations of distress swelled my heart, and so pressed on my brain, that I had suddenly to leave the room, pretending I was wanted at the mines.

I walked to an unoccupied building adjoining the Terhee Kothee, (which was outside the original defences,) and concealed in one of the cellars, I vainly struggled to convince myself that it *must* be done, till the convulsions of my heart were relieved by tears. O my God, what a trial! I could have faced death in its most appalling form without a tremor, but this separation from my family, who would be utterly destitute by my death, weakened my resolution, and I sorrowfully resolved to stay. The sacrifice might involve me, and them, perhaps; for if I fell in the hazardous undertaking, who would think of the family of him whom the world would call a fool? The disinterested motives which had influenced me would doubtless be impugned, and my family gain little by their relationship to me. I could not stipulate for a reward for myself, or a provision for them, because it would have stripped my devotion of all its unselfishness.

Instead of returning home I went into the apartment near the Great Gate of the Residency, where Major North and Lieutenant Sewell were busy preparing Enfield ammunition. There the coming relief was the topic at once introduced. Strange to say, that in a quarter of an hour I left them, resolved to do my duty, without their perceiving that, while joyously conversing with them, I was in reality deliberating upon the fate of my family, and deciding between life and death!

I endeavoured, without exciting suspicion, to discover whether a permanent dye was procurable in the retrenchment; and, luckily for my little beauty, there was none. I obtained a complete Oriental suit by borrowing each article from separate natives; and, tying them in a bundle, took them home. I remained quite composed till six o'clock in the evening, when, as was customary with me, I kissed the family, and left, pretending that I was for duty at the mines, and that I might be detained till late in the morning. I carried my bundle to a small room in the slaughter-yard, and was there dressed by that good, steady young man, Mr. F. Quieros, whom I enjoined to keep it a secret for the present. I was amused at my own ugliness as I carefully surveyed each feature in the glass to see that the colouring was well spread. I did not think that the shade of black was quite natural, and I felt somewhat uneasy about it, till we talked over the chances of detection, and came to the conclusion that the darkness of the night was favourable to me. Kunoujee Lal now joined us, and seemed to chuckle at the ridiculous appearance of the metamorphosed Sahib, as we walked over together to the quarters of Sir James Outram.

Natives are not permitted to go into the house of a European with shoes on, nor to take a seat uninvited. In order to draw particular attention to myself I did both, and the eyes of the officers, who sat at the General's table, were at once turned angrily and inquiringly upon the queer man who did such impudent things. Questions and answers were exchanged without detecting the disguise, although my plain features were known to every one of the outraged officers; who called in the General, and he took some time to recognise me. I regarded this first step in the adventure as presaging success, and was glad to lay hold on any little thing to keep up my confidence. I was daubed once more by the General himself, and, considering where I was going to, there was extraordinary hilarity in the whole proceeding, which was most beneficial to my nerves. My turban was readjusted; my habiliments subjected to a close inspection; and my waistband adorned by a loaded double-barrelled pistol, (belonging to the gallant and amiable Captain Sitwell, A.D.C.), which was intended for myself should there be no possibility of escaping death at the hands of the mutineers, who would have done it in their own particular way.

At half-past eight o'clock our gaiety ceased, for that

was the time appointed to leave. The kind-hearted and chivalrous Sir James, and my good friend Colonel Napier, pressed my hand, with a few encouraging words; the rest, with many earnest prayers for my success, shook hands; and I started with Kunoujee Lal, in the company of the brave Captain Hardinge, who came down to the picquet, on the river Goompty, to pass me out. As I parted from him he tightly squeezed my hand, as if much affected, and slowly observed, that he would give his life to be able to perform what I was doing. His last encouraging and cheering words were feelingly addressed to me, "NOBLE FELLOW! YOU WILL NEVER BE FORGOTTEN!"

CHAPTER XI.

Courage chilled in the water—A shivering matchlockman—Examined by a native officer—Too much light, and dangerous jostling—A watchman's challenge—No one talks of the English!—Everything wrong in the dark—A walk round the enemy—A gallant guide frightened—An old cultivator, and a young one—The dogs bark—Skinned toes—Hide and go seek—A young woman's thigh squeezed in the dark—A careless Sepoy guard questioned by its enemy—Alum Bagh avoided—A dreadful surprise—Sepoys tell us the way to a swamp, and we go into it—A fatiguing struggle to keep two heads above water—An angry man—Passing between two fires—Villagers flying for safety—A topographical sketch on the sands all wrong—A sleeper disturbed.

The night was dark—the sky without a cloud—and there was nothing to guide us but the bright mysterious stars, and a few lights flickering across the river. On our right lay the lines of the enemy, extending past the palaces to the bridge of boats, and on the left they crowded towards the elegant iron bridge, and the old stone bridge beyond, over which we were to recross the river that flowed calmly and silently before us, and divided the two armies. I descended naked to the stream, with the clothes on my head rolled into a bundle. The first plunge into the lines of the enemy, and the cold water, chilled my courage immensely, and if the guide had been within reach I should, perhaps, have pulled him back, and given up the enterprize. But he waded quickly through the river, and reaching the opposite shore, went crouching up a trench for about three hundred yards, to a grove of low trees on the edge of a pond, where we paused to dress. We were interrupted for a few minutes by a man coming down to wash: he went away without observing us, who would if we could, have lain as close to the earth as the leaves under us, for he must have seen both had his eyes turned our way. My confidence now returned, and with my sword resting on the shoulder, we advanced into the huts in our front, where we met a matchlock-man. I thought it prudent to be the first to speak, and remarked, as we approached, that the night was cold, and after his repeating that it *was* cold, I passed on, observing that it would be colder by-and-bye.

Proceeding six or seven hundred yards further, we reached the iron bridge over the Goompty, where we were stopped, and called over by a native officer who sat in an upper-storied house, and seemed to be in command of a cavalry picquet whose horses were saddled. My guide advanced to the light, and I stayed a little back in the shade. We said that we had come from Mundeon, (our old cantonment, then in possession of the enemy), and that we were going into the city to our homes. We continued on along the left bank of the river to the stone bridge, (about eight or nine hundred yards from the iron bridge,) passing unnoticed through a number of Sepoys and matchlock-men, some of whom were escorting persons of rank in palankeens, preceded by torches. There was more light than I cared for, and I would have given much to have had perfect darkness throughout the city. Recrossing the Goompty by the stone bridge, we glided by a sentry, (who was closely questioning a dirtily-dressed native,) into the Chouk, or principal street of the city of Lucknow, which, to my great relief, was not illuminated so much as it used to be previous to the siege, nor was it so crowded. I shuffled and jostled against several armed men in the street without being spoken to, and only met one guard of seven Sepoys, who were amusing themselves with women of pleasure.

Kunoujee Lal made several attempts to leave the main street, and wander through the dark and narrow turnings; but I resisted his wish to avoid the crowd, feeling sure that our safety lay in courting inquiry. When about to issue into the country, we were challenged by a watchman, who merely asked what we were. The part of the city traversed by us that night seemed to have been deserted by at least a third of its inhabitants, and I did not hear a single reference to the English the whole way!

I was in great spirits when we reached the green fields, into which I had not been for five months. Every plant was fragrant, and the smell of the fields refreshing. I greedily sniffed it all as I devoured a delicious fresh carrot, and gave vent to my feelings in a conversation with Kunoujee Lal, who joined in admiring the luxuriance of Oudh, and lamented with me that it was now in the hands of wretches whose rapacity and misgovernment were ruining it.

The environs of the city were beautifully wooded, and planted with fruit and flower trees, through which we could scarce see our direction. But we went onwards in high spirits, and accomplished four or five miles without suspecting the trouble before us. We had taken the wrong road, and were now quite out of the way, in the Dilkooshah Park, which was occupied by the enemy! As this was the route we were to return I thought I ought not to lose the chance thus afforded of examining the position; and leaving Kunoujee Lal seated in the shade of a large tree, I walked round it. On rejoining the guide I found him in great alarm; the thought had occurred that I would distrust him because of the mistake, which, he urged, was occasioned by anxiety to take me away from the picquets of the enemy. I bade him not to be frightened, for I was not annoyed, as such accidents are not unfrequent in the dark, even when there is no danger to be avoided.

It was now about midnight. Near a village we saw a cultivator watching his crop, and endeavoured to persuade him to show us the way for a short distance, but he urged old age and lameness. Another, whom I peremptorily told to come with us, ran off screaming, and alarmed the dogs of the village, which made us run quickly into the canal flowing under the Charr Bagh. I fell several times in our flight, owing to wet and slippery shoes, and sore feet. The shoes being hard and tight, had rubbed the skin off my toes, and cut into the heels. We crouched in the bed of the stream till the alarm subsided, when we entered another village for a guide. The whole ground was so cut up by ravines, and barred by garden walls, that we made no progress through it; and there was reason to fear that we might awkwardly stumble on one of the many parties of troops in the neighbourhood, which, the old cultivator told us, had been that day withdrawn from the front. I entered a wretched hut, and groping in the dark for an occupant, pressed the soft thigh of a woman, who started, but heeded my earnest whisper to be quiet. The good-natured creature woke her mother;

and both put us on the right road, and blabbed all they knew of the proceedings of the enemy, who seemed to be bragging greatly after the retrograde movement.

About one o'clock we reached an advanced picquet of Sepoys, who told us the way, after asking where we had come from and whither we were going. They executed the duty most clumsily and carelessly. I thought it safer to go to the picquet than to try to pass unobserved. Kunoujee Lal now begged I would not press him to take me into the Alum Bagh. He described it as surrounded by rifle pits and mutineers, who were sure to arrest us if detected passing over to the English garrison; and he urged that, as he had not been there, it would be hazarding too much to attempt to reach it. I was tired and in pain, and would, therefore, have preferred going in; but, as he feared it, I desired him to go on to the camp of the Commander-in-Chief, which he said was on the Cawnpoor road, near Bunnee, a village eighteen miles from Lucknow.

By three o'clock we reached a grove of mangoe trees, situated on a plain, in which a man was singing at the top of his voice. I thought he was a villager; but he got alarmed on hearing us approach, and astonished us by calling out a guard of Sepoys, all of whom asked questions. It was an anxious moment. Kunoujee Lal lost heart for the first time, and threw away the despatch entrusted to him for Sir Colin Campbell. I drew their attention to his fright, and begged they would not terrify poor travellers, unaccustomed to be questioned by so many valorous soldiers; they ceased their chatter, and we replied to the enquiries of the officer that we were going to Umroula, (a village two miles this side of the Commander-in-Chief's camp), to inform a friend of the death of his brother by a shot from the British entrenchment at Lucknow. They were greatly relieved on discovering that they had been falsely alarmed, for their terrible foe was only a few miles distant.

We took the direction indicated by them, and after walking for half an hour, disappeared in a jheel, or swamp, which are large and numerous in Oudh. We waded onwards up to our waists, and sometimes to our necks in water, checked at every step. Before we found that we were in a jheel, we had gone too far to recede. It was a long and tiresome struggle, and we were doubtful whether we should ever get out of it. The mud and high reeds clung to us, sometimes holding back a shoe, a stocking, or the scabbard of my sword, and now and then drawing the scarf from my shoulders. My guide being a little man, had occasionally to be held by the neck to keep his head above water. Indians rarely give expression to disappointment in curses, and the good fellow bore the interruptions more patiently than I did. Indeed, he was once or twice disposed to laugh at the vehemence with which I abused every mutineer, every weed, every bit of mud, and every drop of water in the province. The colour was gone from my hands, and I feared there would be little left upon my countenance, which would then have been the death of me. After two hours of intense labour and anxiety we landed, and, despite of the remonstrances of Kunoujee Lal, I rested for a quarter of an hour.

Being again doubtful of the road, we entered a village and went on to the *Chubootra*, or village office, where several men were sleeping outside on cots. Kunoujee Lal woke one; but he refused to go with us, and spoke contemptuously of the enemy, on hearing we were sent by Raja Man Singh to ascertain the strength and whereabouts of the English dogs.

"Have you not heard that from the fellows who ran from them? Go away! and do not disturb our rest."

We departed from the angry man in haste, dreading that further perseverance might involve us in trouble by waking the other sleepers.

The moon shone brightly, and the firmament sparkled with stars as we pressed forward over an extensive plain. We came on two more guards, about three hundred yards asunder, seated with their heels to the fire. I did not care to face them, and passed between the two flames unnoticed, for the careless men had no sentries thrown out. A little later we met several villagers, with their families and chattels mounted on buffaloes, and we learnt from them that they were flying for their lives from the English, who, they said, were murdering and plundering all around them. The frightened creatures were in such a hurry that they would not stop to tell us more, for we would have asked a thousand questions in our great joy. By drawing lines on the sand we settled the probable whereabouts of the troops, and then started off in the wrong direction, and were only stopped going over to the enemy again by missing the bustling noise of the camp, for which we listened. It was about four o'clock in the morning when we stopped at the corner of a grove, where I lay down, fatigued, to sleep for an hour. Kunoujee Lal entreated I would not do so, but I thought he overrated the danger, and desired him to go into the grove to see if there was any one there who could guide us. He had not gone far when I was startled by the challenge, in a native accent, WHO COMES THERE?

CHAPTER XII.

A British picquet surprised—Goldie, and brandy—Dick and his pony—Lieut. Vaughan puzzled—Dialogue with Sir Colin Campbell—A useful note of recommendation—Thanks to the Almighty and to the guide—Modern heroes better than old ones—Arrival announced to Residency—Knights of chivalry and the ladies—A hearty meal and a strange story, in good company—What Sir Colin Campbell is like—An attempt to see a Review from the back of a horse—Advance to the Alum Bagh, and a little battle—An unintelligible telegram—Advance to the Martiniere College—A dangerous look at a bridge—A bonfire for the Residency—The grave of Claude Martin—The enemy wide-awake, and Sir Colin asleep.

KUNOUJEE LAL started too on hearing the challenge, for we had not the remotest idea of there being a guard within a few paces of us. I listened attentively to catch the words that fell from the sentry and the replies of my companion, who adroitly tried to discover to which army the picquet belonged, without compromising his own safety. The entire guard turned out, and so many voices soon disclosed to him that we had reached the British lines! He informed them that he was accompanied by an English officer, which increased their suspicion; and it was not till I shook the Siekh commander heartily by the hand that Kunoujee Lal was believed. I could scarcely realize the fact that I was safe, for my mind having been at full stretch and tuned, as it were, to a particular chord the whole night, it could not readily resume its usual tone.

The native officer gave me an escort of two Sowars, after many expressions of wonder at my temerity, and

I started for the advance guard. Midway a horseman, who rode at full speed, turned to stop us; and I had the pleasure of making myself known to Lieutenant Goldie, of the 9th Lancers, who took me to his tent, gave me dry stockings and trousers, and a glass of brandy, which my shivering body greatly needed. Cold and fatigue vanished under its generous warmth, but it did not compose my thoughts, which ran wild in and out of the mazes of fancy, still striking on the night strings. Captain Dick, of the 29th Foot, (who commanded the infantry of the advance guard,) was roused from a delicious slumber, and, on learning the cause of the intrusion, at once put me on his fine Burmah pony, and walked by my side to within a quarter of a mile of the camp, where I dismounted.

It was five o'clock, and the sun rose majestically into a beautiful blue, clear, sky. It shone that morning on as strange a looking creature as ever met the eye of a naval officer; and it was not singular that Lieutenant Vaughan should stare at him through his glass as he asked the way to the tent of the Commander-in-Chief. That officer, besides being very clever and very fearless, is very civil; and on hearing from whence I came, he unhesitatingly stepped before me, as I often afterwards saw him step before the enemy, and in a couple of minutes the tent was reached. As I approached the door an elderly gentleman with a stern face came out, and going up to him, I asked for Sir Colin Campbell.

"I am Sir Colin Campbell!" was the sharp reply, "and who are you?"

I pulled off my turban, and, opening the folds, took out a short note of introduction from Sir James Outram.

"This, sir, will explain who I am, and from whence

I came." It was impetuously read, his piercing eyes being raised to my face almost at every line.

"Is it true?" he asked.

"I hope, sir, you do not doubt the authenticity of the note?"

"No!—I do not!—but it is surprising! How did you do it?"

I was tired, and anxious to be left alone to my thoughts, and I begged of Sir Colin to excuse my telling the story then, and to put me to bed.

I was put into the bed of Sir David Baird; the tent was carefully darkened; and, away from all but the eye of the Almighty, I knelt and returned most heart-felt thanks for my escape from the dreadful perils of the night. I was greatly indebted to my intelligent guide, who let me speak as seldom as possible, and throughout evinced amazing wit and courage. I should not have succeeded without the assistance of this faithful man; and I grieve to say that his good services upon this and upon several other occasions have been inadequately rewarded.

The most delicious visions of the future lingered in my mind as I thought of the success of the enterprize. For less than this, names have descended from age to age as if never to be obliterated from the heroic pages of history.

Aristomenes ventured alone, at night, to the city of Sparta, in a spirit of defiance, and fixed a shield on the temple of Minerva, with an inscription that he dedicated it to the goddess from the spoils of the Spartans. The renown of Horatius is greater now than when he defended the passage against the Etruscans, whilst the last beams of the bridge fell clashing into the river, to save his friends. The Romans nobly honoured him with a statue, and as much land as he could plough round in a day; and every Roman subscribed the cost of a day's food to reward him. The noble Mucius, to deliver his country of a dangerous enemy, passed into the camp of Porsena to kill him, and when brought before the king he thrust his hand into the fire, and held it in the flame with unmoved countenance, exclaiming,—"See how little thy tortures can avail to make a brave man tell the secrets committed to him!" The world has not yet forgotten the wild devotion of Decius and his son, who, owing to the issue of an ominous dream, devoted themselves to the gods of death, and dashed into the ranks of the enemy, to be slain for the salvation of their country.

Aristomenes did a mere act of bravado. The desperate courage and devotion of Horatius Cocles were excited in the heat of battle. The noble Mucius was one of three hundred who vowed to kill Porsena and the lot fell to him. The extravagant zeal of Decius and his son was provoked by shame and superstition. Yet the fame of their deeds has reached through the ruin of ages to excite us to similar daring. Should I be remembered when the records of centuries are condensed for the instruction of youth? Should I be honored with a statue, and would every Englishman subscribe the cost of a day's food to reward me?

Before quitting Sir James Outram it was agreed that my arrival should be announced by hoisting the flag of the semaphore in the Alum Bagh. When retiring to the bed of the aide-de-camp, I prayed Sir Colin Campbell to have that done, as soon as possible, lest my wife should hear of my absence before the intelligence of my safety, which would have endangered her health, if the discovery did not destroy her affectionate heart. The fear that she and my children might be left destitute by my death had distressed me throughout the night, and it was a relief to know, now, that if killed in the hazardous duty of guiding the troops to the relief of the garrison, I had done enough to secure a provision for them.

The old Knights of Chivalry despised every thing sordid and mean, and deemed nothing so glorious as recovering virtuous and beautiful females from wicked monsters. Would the good, the patient, and the lovely women of Lucknow, remember one who had ventured so much to deliver them from the dark-skinned monsters? I hoped so; for few favors please so much as those which come in enchanting showers from the soft lips and brilliant eyes of women: than whom no one is better suited for soothing the timid and encouraging the brave.

Sir Colin Campbell good naturedly took so much trouble to keep out the light from my tent, that I could not have slept even if sufficiently composed to do so. Between ten and eleven o'clock I breakfasted with him and his staff, who attentively listened to my story while I greedily devoured a large share of everything on a plentiful table, now and then parenthetically observing that there was nothing comparable to bread and butter; that eggs and bacon was a fit dish for a king; Scotch marmalade food for gods; and coffee, *with milk and sugar*, a most refreshing beverage. Picture to yourself, reader, a sweep who had made an attempt to wipe himself clean, and you will have an idea of the hideous creature who sat before Sir Colin and his laughing staff of young scamps, swallowing all the delicacies before him.

His Excellency kept me shut up with himself, repeatedly enjoining me to say nothing on the subject of the relief to the officers of the camp, who he observed would endeavour to extract all I knew, and then form *their* notions of what was right and wrong, and spread injurious stories of his own projects. The power of secrecy did not escape the acuteness of Sir Colin Campbell, who enforced it on all admitted to his confidence; and, when it was his wish to do so, he succeeded, more than most men, in artfully misleading persons as to his designs. He did me the honour of freely discussing with me the scheme forwarded to him by Sir James Outram for his consideration; and I was particularly struck by his quick perception of everything, and the promptitude with which he mastered the strong and assailible points of the city.

I am no great authority, but I may venture to state that the whole bias of his mind seemed to me to be essentially martial, and on that subject remarkably discoursive. He is shrewd in his perception of character; unmercifully rejects all silliness and imbecility; quickly recognises the meritorious, but slowly rewards them. He is active and ardent, and perhaps too vehement under excitement, when he says rather disorderly things for small faults, and only makes amends by quickly forgetting them. When he chooses, he can enchant by his agreeable frankness and familiarity, and the most interesting anecdotical conversation, when his sharp and severe features relax into unaffected sweetness, and his piercing eyes sparkle with humour. In the field of action he is seen to perfection, for his ruling passion is aroused. He is there ubiquitous, and his quick eye seems to see everything, and his intrepid heart to be unmoved by the dangers into which his impetuous will recklessly leads it.

The following afternoon the Commander-in-Chief reviewed the troops, and being anxious to see the gallant little force, I accompanied him on a young untrained horse that flew about the plain as if I were a stinging fly on his back. I ineffectually made several desperate efforts to stay with the cavalcade of staff officers, and catch the harangues which His Excellency screamed out to each regiment as he stopped before it. The provoking beast started and wriggled at the sight of every one of the fine fellows, who were rending the air with hurrahs at the close of those martial orations, which made little of the enemy, and much of themselves; and, at last growing impatient of the whole thing, he snorted at a couple of hamlets in the distance, and scampered home, quite careless of the vicious exertions I made to prevent him. That was, indeed, a fit horse for a Commander-in-Chief, who did not care whither he went, and was as intractable as itself!

There were over four thousand troops on the ground, and as I surveyed the whole line, I felt that the difficult and dangerous task before them would be accomplished, and reflected with pride that I was to guide them. The following morning the first movement was made to the Alum Bagh. The 93rd Highlanders had the post of honour at the head of the column, and were marching joyously to the charming Scotch tune of *Castles in the Air*, when two shots from guns on our right disabled six of them. Sir Colin was instantly out with calvalry and horse artillery, and rapidly advanced upon the enemy, who limbered up and attempted to escape, as Lieutenaut Gough fell upon them with his Siekh horse; and, after a sharp conflict, in which he greatly distinguished himself, captured the guns. Sir Colin crossed a morass to the dilapidated fort of Jelelabad, (where the enemy were supposed to have their powder manufactory), and, whilst he examined the place through his glass, a musketry fire, from an incredible distance, fell harmlessly hundreds of yards from us. The column meanwhile went on, and we rejoined it as it neared the Alum Bagh, without further hindrance.

Before the arrival of Colonel Little, of the 9th Lancers, (who had been sent in on the morning of the 10th November with the message announcing my safety), Sir James Outram had signalled "Has Kavanagh arrived?" and been answered "Unintelligible," which occasioned intense anxiety in the garrison, till the welcome news was telegraphed about twelve o'clock A.M., when my wife was informed of my adventure, and felt—as every good woman feels when her husband does his duty. The enormity of the danger I had encountered—the fearful fate which might have befallen her and the children—the ecstatic feeling that her husband had ventured so much for the public weal, stupified her as the sensations of each crowded into her suffering mind, for her health was bad. She had only a few days previously been almost frightened out of her wits by a severe round shot wound in the leg.*

* Mrs. Kavanagh was severely wounded, during the siege of Lucknow, in the leg, by a round shot, which produced a very serious contusion. Mrs. Kavanagh also suffered severely from the hardships of the siege, and I had occasion to attend her for several attacks.—*Certificate by Dr. H. M. Greenhow, Assistant Surgeon, H.M. Bengal Army.*

On the morning of the 14th November, the second move for the relief of the garrison was made from the Alum Bagh, to the Dilkooshah Park, through highly cultivated fields, and numerous groves of trees; which would have afforded excellent shelter to the sharpshooters of the enemy, had they ventured to do more than eye our compact little force from the roofs of distant houses in the suburbs of the city. At the palace in the park, a few mutineers and matchlock-men showed themselves, and kept up a desultory fire. Our artillery opened upon them, and the glorious 53rd regiment started in pursuit, and followed till they reached the slope leading to the Martiniere College, where they were stopped by a well-directed fire from three or four guns. Sir Colin only stayed till I described the features of the ground, when he descended upon the enemy occupying the intervening space, despite of a heavy fire from the Martiniere as our skirmishers issued from the bushy cover on to the plateau. The mutineers retreated across the canal, and made a strong demonstration of assailing us over the bridge. They were checked by the rifles of the Highlanders, and the fire of a battery of heavy guns, and soon after were disconcerted by an unpremeditated rush over the canal by the 53rd regiment, who were most difficult to hold, and the Punjab Infantry, under the gallant Green, who were very impetuous.

Sir Colin had previously reconnoitred the left end of the canal, where there was a large masonry bridge; and, as I could not tell whether it was entire, I rode under the shelter of a ravine within a hundred yards of the bridge, and brought back intelligence that it seemed to be so Sir Colin, who had examined it through his glass from the other side, remarked that it looked to him to be broken; whereupon I observed that not having seen the roadway, I could not be sure. "Why not assure yourself of it?" inconsiderately spoke General Mansfield, for the enemy were posted behind it. "I can do that too," I replied, and rode over to the bridge, in the face of a close fire, and returned with my horse severely wounded. Two arches of the bridge were broken, and, on the left, the canal was dammed up, so as to make it unfordable under Bankes's Bungalow, the direction the enemy expected us to go.

The Commander-in-Chief himself saw, before it was dark, that the troops were properly disposed, and they passed the night tentless, with their arms by their side. Captain Alison and myself lit a bonfire upon the highest point of the College, to announce the arrival of Sir Colin, and to signal to Sir James Outram to sally out the following morning and occupy some of the intervening buildings, so as to facilitate the relief. Sir David Baird afterwards descended with me to the vault containing the remains of Claude Martin, the remarkable founder of the College, in order to learn whether the tomb had been respected. We found broken in two pieces the marble slab with the modest epitaph "Here lie the remains of Claude Martin, who came to India a private soldier, in 1760, and died a Major-General in 1800, A.D." The marble bust of him when he was old, and a plaster bust of Martin, when he was a young man, were scattered in pieces with his bones, which had been disinterred. We respectfully buried them, and Sir David carried away the face of the second bust.

It was a cold, dark, night. Our wretched foe did nothing to disturb the repose we greatly needed, and they doubtless spent the whole time in vowing to each other that we should not do it! Sir Colin lay on the cold floor, dreaming of the coming battle, and the voice of the "people of England," which was to point to him as the man who did it! I humbly lay by his side, and dreamt too.

CHAPTER XIII.

Sir Colin's look at Lucknow—A new route proposed—A dangerous passage passed—Saved a wounded soldier—Chivalry of Lord Seymour—In at the roof Highlanders!—Assault on the Secunder Bagh—Captains Cooper and Burroughs—The 53rd Foot would go in—Frightful slaughter—Colonel Ewart and the enemy's damned colours—The Shah Nujiff Mausoleum—Peel and Middleton knock for admittance—First assault repulsed—Major Alison—Captured by Adrian Hope—A glorious old soldier surrounded by his fine staff—General Mansfield.

SIR COLIN CAMPBELL is a short sleeper, and he rises half dressed; his toilet is the shortest possible, and he is usually the first in the saddle, and the last out of it. At early dawn he visited the several posts, and inspected the approach to the Residency proposed by Sir James Outram. From the pinnacle of the Martiniere College he afterwards surveyed the city spread broadly before us, with its glittering domes, white temples, long tortuous streets, and embowered palaces; and he did not descend till minutely informed of the situation of the several positions intervening. His eagle eye embraced the remarkable features of Lucknow, and he asked pertinent questions respecting them. I was opposed to the route proposed hence by Sir James Outram, because it had been followed before by Havelock, and was, therefore, sure to be lined by loop-holed defences. I suggested a passage more to the right, between the river and the canal, as not likely to be prepared for resistance, and as affording a good approach for a surprise.

During the day, the enemy came out in large numbers to threaten our position at the Martiniere, by my proposed road. The infantry marched slowly through the woods and ripening crops in small detached parties, and halted, wherever they liked, in separate groups. The cavalry slowly joined the disorderly procession, few and far between, while light and heavy guns laboured through the sands. There seemed to be no directing head, and no preconcerted plan of attack. The cavalry scampered and capered over the plain, flourishing their swords at a great distance from our force, a part of which was quickly and quietly forming up in the dry bed of the canal. Their artillery blazed away, under cover of the woods, with some precision and much obstinacy, till the British infantry and cavalry mounted the high bank of the canal, when the rebel force, after a ludicrous show of resistance, turned about, and went fast homewards in the same irregular order.

Sir Colin Campbell followed some distance to see and understand more of the ground through which I proposed to conduct him. He returned, satisfied that it was practicable, and his dispositions for our advance the following morning were promptly made. His Excellency massed the artillery on the left flank, and maintained a heavy cannonade all night, to impress the enemy with the belief that he would pursue the old route.

The advance was made so silently and skilfully that the enemy could not attempt to occupy the ground over which we quickly passed. Nearly the whole distance was through narrow tortuous lanes, or low thick plantations enclosed by mud walls; which afforded such admirable shelter, that Sir Colin was amazed at the good fortune that let him pass unmolested. Indeed, the natural obstacles were so great that some cheeks blanched at the contemplation of them. Near the Secunder Bagh I captured a man escaping through a lane, and learnt from him that the garden was strongly occupied, and that the enemy were completely surprised by this unexpected movement on their rear. I explained to the Chief his position, and respectfully advised the immediate advance of artillery to secure the gateway. A few mutineers were seen in the lanes on our left, who disappeared the moment the skirmishers of the 53rd and 93rd regiments showed themselves.

A terrific fire of musketry poured from the high walls as some of the 53rd Foot, with Sir Colin, reached the angle of the garden facing the river. The first man who attempted to pass under it was severely wounded in the hip, and lay with bullets ploughing the earth around him. I leaped from my horse, and dragged him by the arms into a hut close by, the poor fellow thankfully squeezing my hands.

With his customary decision Sir Colin directed the 53rd Foot to line a shallow trench, by which retreat to the bridge of boats over the river was cut off. A gentleman by his side mistaking the order to mean an assault, suddenly sprang forward on his small slender horse, and, with drawn sword, remained calling to the men to follow him, exposed to a close destructive fire. It was the handsome youth whose white passive features had just attracted my notice, as he joined the staff; the fiery and impetuous young man was the same who looked so sedate and so unexcitable only a minute before.

The suddenness of this startling exhibition of spirit excited the lookers on, and the 53rd Foot, (who needed very little calling,) were passionately rising for the assault, when Sir Colin checked them in a loud voice.

"Come back! come back Lord Seymour; you have no business there! I did not order it! I witnessed your gallantry with great pleasure. Consider yourself, my lord, as attached to my staff for the present! I admire your noble spirit, and must take care of you!"

The young nobleman returned abashed, and looking as if it was nothing to have escaped the hundred bullets directed at him.

Meanwhile, the artillery passed at a gallop, and, in superb style, mounted a high embankment, which gave them the command of the gate, and deprived the rebels of the only means left of escaping the terrible doom impending. The fire from the walls increased in fierceness as the Highlanders pressed forward, with some of the 53rd foot, to clear the huts in the neighbourhood. Sir Colin rode under the muskets of the enemy, impetuously directing every move. More and more the fusilade increased, and our intrepid fellows fell fast to the ground. The excited artillery persevered in a rapid and well-directed fire against the nearest tower. The noise grew deafening. Two companies of the Highlanders, with fixed bayonets, mounted to the plateau before the garden, and rushed upon the enemy, concealed in an extensive range of houses, who molested our flank. A dead wall stopped them.

"In at the roof! Tear off the tiles and go in through the roof, Highlanders!" roared the old Chief.

In an instant bonnets and kilts disappeared through smashed tiles, torn mats, and broken bamboos, and the enemy were pursued to the barracks, where Captain Stewart furiously fell upon a couple of guns and captured them.

The noisy contest reverberated through the whole neighbourhood, and the earth trembled under the wheels of the cannon, as they belched forth shot and shell. Sir Colin Campbell and his gallant staff moved in the midst of it, protected by a miracle. The brave tawny Siekhs reached the front; the breach in the Secunder Bagh was declared practicable; a hole barely large enough for a single man was visible.

> This day, this dreadful day, let each contend;
> No rest, no respite, till the shades descend;
> Till darkness, or till death shall cover all:
> Let the war bleed, and let the mighty fall!
> Till bathed in sweat be every manly breast,
> With the huge shield let each brawny arm deprest,
> Each aching nerve refuse the lance to throw,
> And each spent courser at the chariot blow.*

The hot and vehement spirit of the undaunted Chief rose, and uncovering his grey hairs, he waved the Siekhs and Highlanders on to the assault. That was a gallant race! The Siekh was first—and dropped in dead! The agitated plumes of a Highland bonnet rose—the wearer stood for an instant in the breach, and fell forward! Another, and another! Two more struggled in the opening to die first. Noble fellows! what cared they for death! Cooper and Burroughs are in, and, followed by their men, they pushed through the tower in pursuit of the mutineers, the mass of whom stood aloof, screened by the shrubs and plants of the garden. The gate was violently forced by the Siekhs, and the enemy dragged dead and dying, and heaped out of the way. The

---

* Pope's Iliad, book II.

assailants pressed in, and the commotion grew fierce and wild to distraction.

Highlanders and Siekhs, besmeared with blood, trampled over the dead, through the plants and houses. Screams and groans ascended above the uproar. Here mutineers manfully received our soldiers on the point of the bayonet—there threw down their muskets, and fiercely defended themselves with swords. Some threw away their arms and pitifully pleaded for mercy to men infuriated by slaughter—others ran to the inner rooms for shelter, and despairingly clutched at the weapons of the fierce soldiers who pressed in after them. Bullets flew in every direction from friend and foe.

The 53rd regiment, encouraged by the gallant Lieutenant Ffrench, violently smashed through the iron bars of a window, and, with loud screams of victory, added to the tumult, the confusion, and the slaughter. Hoarse calls for help came rom this side—loud and frequent orders to go in and bayonet rom the other—curses, in the most awful words, mingled with imploring voices. A few ran wild through the combatants to end their misery by death. Hundreds were deliberately bayoneted, and pitched, writhing in the agonies of death, into a reservoir. The appalling sounds of cutting, hacking, and stabbing, were heard all round the garden, with the dreadful screams of the combatants. "CAWNPOOR, boys! Remember our women and children! Mercy! No mercy for you!" Miserable creatures! a day of retribution had come.

The mass of dark men moved here, there, backwards, and forwards, trampling down the plants that sent forth their fragrance to nostrils choked with blood—many ran in and out of the rooms, pursued by their fearless and merciless foe. The scene was animated and horrible to the utmost degree, when the effect was increased by a conflagration, from which the mutineers struggled on to our weapons, and were thrown back upon the raging flames! Some wretches, as a last resource, sought concealment on the roofs and in the towers, where they were remorselessly followed and chucked dying to the yard below! The strife was obstinately maintained at one tower. Officers and men courageously threw themselves against the door to burst it, and were killed; and another, and another fell in fruitless efforts to enter. Artillery were brought in, and the awful uproar was made more awful by its booming and by crashing walls, as the balls passed through the room of the desperate defenders.

At last the tumult ceased, and the victors walked triumphantly through the blood of the prostrate foe to count their bodies. Two thousand of the enemy covered the ground, lapped one in the other: they were either dead or dying. At one spot the corpses above were moved up and down by the suffocating respirations of the living below! Animate and inanimate nature alike lay bruised on the ground.—The eye encountered dreadful scenes of carnage all over the enclosure.—Seven Europeans effected their escape from the massacres of Seetapoor and Mahomdee, and threw themselves on the protection of the Chief of Mythowlee, who treacherously surrendered them to the Begum at Lucknow. Almost at the time that the atrocities of Cawnpoor were being avenged in the Secunder Bagh, four of the English captives* were dragged from their

* Sir M. Jackson, Captain Patrick Orr, Lieutenant Burnes, (a brother of Sir Alexander, who was murdered at Cabool,) and Serjeant-Major Morton.

prison, bound arm to arm, and barbarously murdered outside the gate of the Kaisur Bagh Palace.

Sir Colin Campbell, mounted on his grey horse, was outside the Secunder Bagh, surrounded by his staff, when a Highland officer, excited, tattered, and blood-stained, issued through the gate, and approached the group with a red banner.

"I have killed the last four of the enemy with my own hand, and here, sir, are their colours!" exclaimed the bleeding and agitated Highlander.

"Damn the colours, sir! Where is your regiment? Go back to your regiment, sir! I thank you Colonel Ewart for your zeal and gallantry, but go back to the regiment!"

The romantic fervour of the intrepid Colonel succumbed to so much practical wisdom from the lips of his great Chief; and as he turned to go I handed him a bonnet, for he had dropped his own in the horrid fray within, where he was foremost among the many daring officers who fought that day.

The artillery bombarded the next position of the enemy in the Shah Sujjiff mausoleum. Captain Peel, cool and calm, rolled forward his ponderous guns before a deadly fire. Major William Middleton, with his lighter guns, passed on the right at a gallop, and unlimbered close under the walls. His fine manly figure could be seen through the smoke, and his loud voice could be heard at intervals encouraging his gallant men. Horses and gunners rolled fast in the sand. The fire redoubled on the side of Peel, while Middleton threw shot and shell at the tower from whence the enemy poured their fatal volleys. It was all in vain. The thick hard walls remained unbroken, and the nerve of the enemy unshaken. The infantry and guns withdrew, and the foe yelled, and made a feint through the gateway of following.

Sir Colin grew anxious for the result, while I exulted that, by the mercy of Providence, I was by his side humbly to dissipate his apprehensions by making little, perhaps too little, of the opposition still in our way. He was equal to the emergency, and his spirit mounted above the difficulties that threatened the success of his operations to relieve the garrison. Highlanders and detachments of other regiments were brought to the front, and, under the shelter of some huts, the Commander-in-Chief passionately reminded them of the noble duty to be executed, and assured them of his confidence that their devoted courage would effect it.

Peel, always cool, clever, and courageous, by extraordinary exertion, dragged his guns up to the tower, as if he were "laying the *Shannon* along side an enemy's frigate."* Brigadier Adrian Hope, and his company of brave Highlanders, approached under a destructive fire from the ramparts. Some of the Chief's staff joined in the assault. The combatants fired fast and furiously—the killed and wounded increased—Major Alison, Military Secretary, received a bullet obliquely through his arm, and I led him to the rear, where it was at once amputated,—officers and men passed by disabled,—our infantry returned the fire without success, and Peel thundered with no result. No one spoke his thoughts, but many feared another repulse. Darkness was fast approaching, and Sir Colin was growing anxious again, when the Highlanders mounted a breach discovered by Adrian Hope, and possessed themselves of this strong

* Sir Colin Campbell's Despatch of the 18th November, 1857.

position, as the enemy swiftly disappeared through a doorway towards the river.

The tall and gaunt Sir Hope Grant was to be seen everywhere throughout the day calmly directing the troops. No amount of locomotion fatigued him, and nothing disturbed his equanimity. Darkness brought no rest for this zealous soldier. Adrian Hope, flushed with victory; Greathead, with the glory of Delhi and his gallant march to Sir Colin encircling his head; the handsome Russell, clever and zealous; and Little, of the immortal 9th Lancers, watched at the head of their brigades, whilst the fierce Leith Hay; the cool and portly Hale; Wells, with the Victoria Cross; the intrepid Gordon, and the valorous Barnston, stood longing for daylight by the side of the 23rd, 53rd, 82nd, 93rd, and detachments of the 64th, 78th, 84th, and 90th Foot, and the 2nd and 4th Punjab Infantry, who were under Captain Green, a distinguished officer, and Lieutenant Willoughby, a promising young man, who was afterwards sacrificed at Rohya by the side of Adrian Hope. Colonel Turner, of the Bengal Horse Artillery, was actively engaged all day, and his intelligent zeal well merited the confidence of his Chief.

The weary troops stood the whole night to their arms, exposed to severe cold, and almost starving. The burning thatched houses in the vicinity threw a soft glare across the plain. Sir Colin lay down late, outside the Secunder Bagh, disturbed by the buzz of large bodies of the enemy who threatened his left flank, and by occasional shots, and the trampling of feet in the garden, as a few of the mutineers attempted to escape through the darkness from their concealment. The glorious old soldier, wrapped in his cloak on the ground, had nobly done his duty through a day of intense trial, and my regard grew stronger as I lay by his side watching his stern, puckered features, moving as if in deep thought.

General Mansfield; Colonel Berkely of the 32nd Foot; Major Alison, Military Secretary; Major Norman, deservedly rising to eminence; the tall and manly Hope Johnstone; swift Alison; quiet Forster; swarthy Metcalfe; and sprightly Sir David Baird, rested around him; the strong and elegant figure of General Mansfield being the most remarkable of all those gallant officers, who had, more or less, suffered during the fighting. He had taken a conspicuous part in the day's proceedings. His calm authoritative demeanour, his handsome person, and intelligent face, indicated the well-bred and accomplished soldier; and it needed little prescience to foresee that he was destined to occupy a prominent place in the affairs of the empire. His varied acquirements and official training fit him eminently for situations of responsibility, and it is a pity that his dignified brevity of manner is misunderstood by persons who overlook his sincerity and earnestness. His cleverness has been of much use to the Commander-in-Chief, who is said to highly appreciate his tact and talents.

CHAPTER XIV.

Naval Brigades' missives to the enemy—The D. D. Bungalows—Ordered to be shot as a spy!—A false colour cut down by Peel—Attack on the Mess House, Observatory, and Motee Mahul Palace—The gallant Worseley of the 90th Foot—Abused by Sir Colin Campbell for a Hibernicism—Worseley and the British banner—A dangerous run to Sir James Outram—A hearty welcome home—Race back to Sir Colin—An unexpected introduction, and a glorious meeting of the Chiefs Outram, Havelock and Campbell—Grand objects of my escape effected—Generous reception by my comrades—A mean reward—Retreat to Cawnpoor—General Wyndham surprised by men on a dog-cart—Reception of the Lucknow refugees at Calcutta.

THE indefatigable Naval Brigade threw shells and rockets into the enemy almost without intermission, and Sir Colin was early on the move again. He made himself acquainted with the localities both sides of the river, and pressed upon the enemy on his left so as to keep clear his communication with the Martiniere. I was sent with Colonel Biddulph, and a detachment of European Infantry and Madras Sappers, under the command of the portly and gallant Colonel Hale, of the 82nd Foot, to take possession of the English houses along the route which had been proposed by Sir James Outram. It was done with little opposition, but through an error of mine it was nearly the death of Colonel Hale; and at one of the Bungalows an order was afterwards issued to shoot me!

Colonel Hale was relieved by a detachment of the

23rd Fusileers. I revisited the Bungalows, and minutely examined the posts of the enemy in that direction. I was not known by sight to any of the new comers, and my singular dress made my position with the army doubtful. My persevering curiosity at last attracted the suspicion of a serjeant, who reported my extraordinary proceedings to Major Bruce, with his opinion that I was a spy of the enemy! I stood in advance of the sentries, and was on the point of running a considerable distance further, when I thought of returning for a glass. Major Bruce then learnt my name, and informed me that he had authorized the serjeant to shoot me if I attempted to approach the mutineers. The return for a glass had saved my life! The gallant and unpretending Colonel Biddulph was afterwards shot at this place.

The enemy were evidently distressed at their reverses and the destructive fire from our heavy guns; and some began to desert to Fyzabad. Sir Colin, pleased at the sight, watched from the towers of the Secunder Bagh the broken lines of citizens and soldiers flying in that direction, and easily augured the alarm produced by his progress thus far. The only positions now to be forced were the buildings known as the "Mess House," the "Observatory," and the "Motee Mahul." The enemy, seeing a Union Jack hoisted by the beleaguered garrison, mounted another near the Kaisur Bagh Palace to mislead us, but I warned the Chief of the artful design, and soon after a shot from Captain Peel cut down the ensign. A force led by Colonel Robert Napier had sallied out of the garrison the day before, and in a very spirited manner forced the defenders from the building known as the "Steam Engine House," and the enclosures adjoining; and Sir James Outram threw shot and shell into those three positions to assist Sir Colin Campbell.

In the afternoon a storming party was formed under the orders of Captain Worseley, of the 90th Foot, who was directed to obey my wishes. The enemy escaped from the Mess House as we rushed into it. From the roof I rapidly examined the strength of the enemy in the Observatory on the left, and the Motee Mahul on our right; and, observing that the former was weakly occupied, and the latter not difficult to capture, I requested Captain Worseley to send twenty-five of his men to the Tara Kothee, who soon cleared it, and to follow me with fifty more. As we leaped from our cover the enemy poured grape and a heavy matchlock-fire from the walls of the Kaisur Bagh, through which we ran two hundred yards. The mutineers met us with a fusilade through the low loop-holes of the Motee Mahul. I suggested that we should seize the loop-holes, but, as I was not understood, I took the rifles of the men, and drove the enemy from three of them; when the artifice being thus explained, the men rushed to the openings, and forced the mutineers from their defences. This gave us the command of the front yard, from which they retired precipitately.

Captain Worseley, gallantly maintained his advantage while I searched outside for a passage to the interior, without succeeding. I returned through the fire from the palace to fetch sappers to break in, and, seeing me run alone, the matchlock-men yelled from the walls and increased their vollies. I remounted my trooper near the Mess House, and was lifting him over the wall to reach Sir Colin, when he observed my haste.

"Where are you going to? What have you done?"

"I ventured, sir, to order Captain Worseley to occupy the Observatory, and I am happy to say that he has captured the Motee Mahul."

"Ah! glad to hear it!"

"But, sir," I continued, "we have not got into it!"

Sir Colin's hasty blood mounted hot to his cheeks, and he almost roared at me, "What do you mean, sir? You first say you have captured the place, and then that you have not got into it! What am I to think of the contradiction? You have told an untruth, sir! I have lost confidence, and will never believe you again!"

His Excellency went on in the angry style I had unwittingly provoked, till I ventured to remind him that I had come for sappers, by whom a passage could be forced in a few minutes. I quickly returned with them, passing a third time, unhurt, through the fire from the palace, which did not miss us all. A breach was soon made; Captain Worseley, who delighted in dash and danger, fell upon the enemy as they tried to escape, and in half an hour he was seen on the top of the inner buildings waving the British banner.

He was a spirited and intelligent officer who needed very little assistance from me, and, the moment I saw him engaged, I withdrew alone to attempt reaching Sir James Outram. I was again under fire till I reached "Martin's House," where I met a soldier of the 64th Foot, from the Residency. In company with him we encountered the fire of the enemy as we ran with all our might towards a group of officers standing under cover of the "Steam Engine House," who looked through their glasses as I rose to the high ground before them. Sir David Baird's cotton quilted tunic, Sir Colin's breeches and felt helmet, and my long jack boots, so altered my appearance, that I reached the group, panting for breath, before being recognised.

"It is Kavanagh! three cheers for him! He is the first to relieve us!"

Reader, if you have never heard the voice of comrades in praise, and felt the hard pressure of the hand that sends the blood leaping to the heart, in the midst of the loud clangor of war, you will not understand the joy that moistened my eyes when such leaders as Outram, Havelock, Napier, and their splendid staff, pressed forward to greet and congratulate my humble self. It was the proudest moment of my life!

"Are you willing, Sir James, to join the Commander-in-Chief at once? The road is clear, but there is that fire from the palace to be encountered."

"Never mind it!" replied Sir James Outram, who turned to the staff and desired them to follow.

Sir James is no runner, and he jogged slowly through the bullets of the enemy, who were greatly excited at the gallant sight. But some of us overdid the run, and scratched our noses in the gravel. Colonel Napier, Lieutenant Sitwell, and the gallant son of Havelock were wounded, and the rest stayed under the corner of the Motee Mahul as the chivalrous Sir James and myself continued onwards. He made poor use of his strong legs, notwithstanding that grape was now added to bullets, and that my inclination was far ahead of myself. Sir James stood in the shade of a hut inside the "Mess House" enclosure, while I searched for the Commander-in-Chief.

"Sir James Outram is waiting, sir, to see you."

"The devil he is! where is he? where has he come from?"

"I have fetched him, Sir Colin, from the Residency, and he is standing yonder."

"Well done! lead the way!"

The Chief followed, and I had the honour of introducing his great brother in arms to our deliverer.

"I am delighted to meet you, Sir James, and I congratulate you on the successful defence of Lucknow."

Sir James complimented the Chief on his brilliant achievement, as he dismounted from his grey charger, and earnestly shook hands.

"Are you prepared, Sir James, to quit the Residency in two hours? Time is precious."

"It is impossible, Sir Colin," replied Sir James, looking surprised at the demand.

"Nothing is impossible, sir!" sharply retorted the impetuous old Chief.

"If you will permit me to explain the reasons for considering it impracticable, you will, Sir Colin, be well satisfied that it cannot be done," deliberately answered Sir James; looking somewhat startled at his Chief's peremptory manner.

"Very well, Sir James, we'll discuss this as early as possible."

He generously turned to speak of me in terms of praise, which I need not repeat. Havelock then approached, and was heartily received by Sir Colin Campbell, as the news passed through the relieving force that the Residency defenders were saved. The whole plain resounded with the roar of artillery, and the proud hurrahs of delight and defiance of our brave deliverers, who crowded forward to witness the affecting meeting of the Chiefs.

This remarkable meeting has been suitably represented

by Mr. T. Jones Barker, in a grand painting styled *The Relief of Lucknow*, which was prepared from drawings made on the spot by Mr. E. Lundgren, for Messrs. Thomas Agnew and Son, of Manchester and Liverpool. The neighbourhood, involved in smoke, and the confusion of the combatants, is so admirably delineated, that while looking at the picture the imagination is involuntarily carried back to the time and the place where Outram and Havelock welcomed the victorious Sir Colin Campbell, in the midst of a splendid staff of officers composed of such leaders as Hope Grant, Mansfield, Peel, V.C., Napier, Inglis, Adrian Hope, Russell, Greathed, Little; and clever and spirited officers like Norman, Moorsom, (abounding in zeal and intelligence,) Alison, Stewart, Johnstone, Probyn, V.C., Watson, V.C., Metcalfe, Forster, Roberts, V.C., and the dashing Anson, also decorated with the Queen's most honorable Cross.

Look again, reader, at the glorious meeting of the Chiefs, and listen to the manly greetings of Havelock, Outram, and the Scotch leader. Observe the pale slender figure in the friendly grasp of the strong stern Highlander. His white hairs have grown gray; his handsome features have been clouded by cares, and illumined by rejoicings; the arm extended to the Chief has waved British troops to victory; and the feeble trembling body has spent its youth, its manhood, and its decline, under the immortal colours of England. His honest heart has throbbed nearly half a century in the service of the State, and this is the last time it is to rejoice at its successes. Havelock is dying! It is his last act in the great drama begun by himself; and, seven days later, he was carried to the grave, with a soul as well prepared for his Maker as the longings of an earnest Christian could make it. His comrades dropped tears upon the earth that covered him, and nations have mourned the loss of a GOOD MAN.

I effected the grand objects of my ambition; I saved many lives,* and, by hastening the relief, gained precious time for Sir Colin Campbell, and his clever coadjutor General Outram, to execute the masterly retreat that rescued the suffering garrison; which obtained for those able officers well-deserved renown; and wrenched Cawnpoor from the grasp of the Gwalior Army that was sorely pressing General Wyndham. In a despatch to the Government of India, the Commander-in-Chief acknowledged my services as follows, "This escape, at a time when the entrenchment was closely invested by a large army, and when communication, even through the medium of natives, was almost impossible, is, in Sir Colin Campbell's opinion, one of the most daring feats ever attempted; and the result was most beneficial, for, in the immediate subsequent advance on Lucknow of the force under the Commander-in-Chief's directions, the thorough acquaintance with the localities possessed by Mr. Kavanagh, and his knowledge of the approaches to the British position, were of the greatest use; and His Excellency desires to record his obligations to this gentleman, who accompanied him throughout

---

* And the public treasure. Two days later, and Sir Colin would have thought no more of abandoning the treasure and jewels, amounting to over £300,000, than he did of capsizing carts loaded with elephants' tusks, which the prize agents had zealously packed for removal. Cawnpoor would have been in such danger, and the retreat so insecure by the delay, that the treasure could not have been fetched away excepting at the risk of sacrificing the army. The Government of India gave me for this, and the other more important services, £2,000! Contrast this with the liberality of the public to Tom Sayers! This spirited fellow will be made comfortable for life for maintaining the British character for pluck in a Prize Ring.

the operations, and was ever present to afford valuable information."

Think, reader, whether great successes like those were worth a paltry life like mine—whether the honourable fame which the world has generously accorded to so humble a creature, was worth so hazardous an adventure? It will be learnt from this narrative that I did not go out as a mere messenger, as some persons have erroneously supposed, but to execute a scheme of my own devising, requiring more than common tact, courage, and intelligence.

My generous comrades had anxiously watched for the announcement of my safety, and welcomed it with an emotion and expression of joy, which filled my soul with intense pleasure. As I re-entered the defences our excellent soldiers pressed forward to welcome me back, and admiring expressions dropped from the lips of the officers as I passed. As I listened to the upbraidings of my weeping wife, and soothed her fond heart, my friends came in "only to look at you!" as some said.

Nothing is comparable to the glory of a good deed, and few things are more gratifying then the sound of manly voices applauding it. Were not greetings like those worth striving for? Was the applause of a world worth the venture of a life exposed to perils that might at any moment extinguish it? Certainly; and when such a service is needed again, men will be found under the Banner of England to do it.

Sir Colin Campbell reached Cawnpoor by forced marches, and arrived in time to preserve his communication, and to reassure the garrison, which was alarmed by failures. The families tremblingly crossed the river by the bridge of boats, through the fire of the enemy, and preparations were made for their safe conduct to Allahabad. I slept in the entrenchment the first night, and in the morning was surprised to find that the regiments from the Crimea were composed of untried youths, who squandered their ammunition on the most insignificant objects. I thought I saw considerable misapprehension as to the proceedings of the enemy, who did not appear to use the advantages surrendered to them.

I purchased a dog-cart and pony, and having occasion to return to the entrenchment the following afternoon with Mr. William Forder, (who did not know where I was taking him,) I drove through a part of the town nearest to the fort where the enemy, it was said, were strongly posted. As I emerged from the houses towards the British defences a stout handsome officer issued from the gateway, apparently vexed, and stopped me.

"May I ask whether you are in possession of your senses?" was the impertinent enquiry.

"Yes!" I answered, "I am in perfect possession of my senses."

"Then do you know where you have been to?"

"Yes; I know perfectly well where I have been."

"Do you know," he continued, "that it is occupied by the enemy?"

"I know very well that it is not, as you have just seen."

"Perhaps," he mockingly observed, "you would like to continue your drive in that direction," pointing to the Assembly Rooms occupied by the enemy, where two officers of the 64th Foot were supposed to be hanging.

"If you consider that any public good is to be gained by my going there in a dog-cart, I am ready to do it," an assertion which brought back the good humour of the officer, who smiled. I passed on to the gate, where the guard he had turned out to the rescue congratulated me on a lucky escape. Further on I learnt that it was General Wyndham to whom I had spoken! The encounter vastly pleased me, for he is a brave officer whom I was most anxious to meet, though I never hoped to surprise him.

We reached Allahabad, and then Calcutta, where the Lucknow refugees and wounded soldiers were welcomed in a suitable manner by Earl Canning and the European population, who crowded to the landing-place to pour forth their generous feelings in hearty cheers as the veiled widows and orphans mounted the carpeted steps, followed by their more fortunate female companions, and the sick, blind, and maimed veterans who had heroically defended them through many a dark night of dangerous toil, and days of intense heat and severe fighting. The crowd kindly gave one more cheer for "Lucknow Kavanagh," as I led my family to the conveyance, which was to carry them home.

CHAPTER XV.

The dark side of the picture—Europeans, Christians, and servants murdered—Captain Savory—Citizens plundered—Moulvie Ahmud-oola interferes and is disgraced—Election of a King—Appointment of Commanders—Civil officers—100,000 assailants—Efforts made to obtain money—Jealousy in the Palace—False reports—The Nana—Havelock's progress—Captives slaughtered—Mutineers pray to be led to Cawnpoor—Subterranean passages to the granaries of the city—Envoy to Delhi Emperor—Havelock's advance to Lucknow—Citizens excited by proclamations—Retreat of the enemy, and panic—Moulvie all-powerful—Relief by Sir Colin Campbell, and rejoicing thereat.

After the capture of Lucknow in March, 1858, I employed an intelligent native to collect information respecting the proceedings of the rebel government during the period we were surrounded by them, and the following summary of his labour will show how the people of Oudh governed themselves after a hundred years experience of the European systems of administration in India. There are separate stages of government for different stages of civilization, and no human exertion can disturb them. Governments advance or retrograde as the people they rule advance or recede in the scale of civilization. The European endeavoured to force the laws of nature upwards, but when his support was withdrawn the whole system fell to the level of the people.

The mutineers, exulting at their success at the battle of Chinut, crossed the river Goompty at different points, and, while some invested the English entrenchment, others spread through the city in search of Europeans and Christians, and persons suspected of being partial to them; most of whom were dragged from their concealment and atrociously murdered. Captain Savory, a retired officer of the Indian service, was one of the victims, who, after surrendering his treasure on the promise of his life, was pulled from his house suffering with rheumatism, and, being unable to walk as fast as his captors, they shot and bayonetted him on the road to the Kaisur Bagh Palace; where the reward subsequently demanded for his hoary head was refused, for he was held in great esteem by the nobility of Lucknow.

The city police were supposed to be staunch supporters of our authority, because they guarded the gallows at the executions before the Old Castle; were seen retreating from Chinut; and fired at the mutineers when they approached their fortified position in the square of the Great Imambarah. The most vindictive pursuit of these unlucky wretches was maintained in the city for several days, and many citizens were shot down only for resembling them. The vagabonds of the city, released from all restraint, plundered the terrified townsmen, encouraged by the soldiery, who, on the pretext of searching for Christians, entered and robbed the houses of the weak and defenceless.

The people, alarmed at the licence of the troops, began to desert the place, and to remove their valuables in the dead of the night. The conservancy establishment, organized by us, dissolved itself, and the accumulation of filth sickened the unfortunate inhabitants. They appealed in vain to the rebel leaders for protection, and the restoration of that order of things which they had a few days before seen extinguished with acclamations of joy. There seemed to be only one leader with the will to help them, and the Moulvie Ahmud-oolla, always anxious to be ackowledged as the head of the Government, warned the troops that they must desist, and appointed police officers, with large rapacious retinues, to enforce his authority. He had it proclaimed that the citizens might put to death all persons attempting to plunder them, and taking up his abode in the beautiful building known as the Observatory, adopted all the airs and ceremonials of royalty. The party in the Palace, annoyed at an impertinence that threatened to arrest their ambitious projects, incited the troops to resent the proclamation, which was particularly directed at them; and the Moulvie was robbed and ignominiously driven from the Observatory, to which he was afterwards only suffered to return at the entreaty of the Mahomedan cavalry. He had not yet obtained the ascendancy over the Hindoo troops that subsequently gave so much trouble to the Begum and her supporters.

The mutineers, wishing to perpetuate their authority, decided upon electing a King, subject to the Emperor at Delhi. This resolution was no sooner known in the Palace, than the Queens began to hold meetings, in which the merits of the different aspirants were angrily discussed, and intrigues concocted for defeating the intention of the troops. The proposal to bestow the Crown on Birjis Kudur was fiercely resented, for he was regarded as the son of a low woman, purchased by Wajid Ali Shah, (the King in captivity,) and seduced before he saw her. But the perseverance of her paramour, Mummoo Khan, and the influence of a large bribe to the "Council of Military Commanders," subdued all opposition, and the boy mounted the throne.

The day of the coronation, mutineers, without distinction of rank, crowded into the Palace and spread through the halls, creating the utmost consternation by their disregard of all decorum, and by their noisy comments on the person and appearance of the lad. Some likened him to a god; some admonished him not to abandon himself to wine, women, and fidlers; and others loudly declared that he was too young and timid, as he stood trembling before the tumultuous crowd of armed men, and started at the report of the muskets discharged close around him in honor of the occasion. The Begum, dreading the violence of the rude and disorganized soldiery, withdrew him to her private apartments, and for awhile bemoaned the bad destiny of her son, whose reign threatened to be a short and dangerous one.

An attempt was made to reduce the troops to some show of subordination by appointing Generals, Brigadiers, Colonels, Majors, and Captains; but as the "Military Council" were well paid by the competitors, this difficult duty was rather slowly performed, and the nominations sometimes resisted by the soldiery, who boasted of being the Alpha and Omega of the whole administration. The civil offices of the city were nominally restored, and plunder stopped, excepting by the officials themselves, who dealt out justice to complainants according to their ability to pay, or the power of the offender to resist. The old regiments were promised more pay, and new levies were raised with great names and little discipline. The Court in the Kaisur Bagh Palace gradually assumed an appearance of splendour, and sent proclamations into the province announcing the extermination of the English, and inviting the Barons to co-operate in restoring the rule of their rightful sovereign. The call was responded to, and, by the close of the first month, the multitude of armed men investing the British entrenchment increased to a hundred thousand, when the streets were overrun by bands of music and numerous banners, with wretchedly mounted cavalcades behind them.

No government can exist without money, especially one composed of the most corrupt and unscrupulous men in the world; and, as the Barons of Oudh were only profuse in promises, raids were made occasionally into the country to fetch in money; bankers were cajoled and threatened; traders were squeezed; the treasures of absent noblemen were dug up from their concealment, and contracts of the revenue sold, for a fourth of their value, to Chukladars, monsters who have always been regarded as the destroyers of Oudh. All these measures, however, failed to fill the treasury, and hence the extraordinary efforts made to replenish it with the sum so zealously guarded inside the Residency, and to force on the troops, and on poor tradesmen, cheques upon the Baillie Guard! Financial embarrassments, and the jealousy and intrigue inherent in native administrations, produced discord in the Palace, and discontent among the troops; and the whole body would have fallen to pieces but for the presence of the resolute band of Englishmen in the Residency.

Several attempts were made to force an entry to them, and the Court thrown into paroxysms of joy and grief by the arrival of messengers, who first reported that the "brave troops" were in, and fiercely fighting hand to hand with the defenders; then that they had reached the magazine and were cutting their way to the much coveted treasure; next that the English, rising from the dead, had cut off the assailants within the Residency; and, lastly, that it was all untrue, for the assailants were safely seated behind the streets, moaning the destruction dealt by the cursed English, who had hurled them back from the barricades. Each disaster infuriated the mutineers, who invariably assailed the Palace and abused the courtiers as friends of the English, or wreaked their disappointment on unresisting tradespeople, by shooting a few in their shops for resisting their arbitrary rates, or disbelieving the story that there were only five Europeans alive in the Residency! Affairs were tending to a dissolution when news reached of the advance of Havelock and the defeat of the Nana of Bithoor, who quickly followed himself. The fiend was refused a royal salute by the Begum, and, therefore, did not enter Lucknow; but his butchers from Cawnpoor implored for permission to assault the British defences, and, the favour being conceded, many did not survive to repeat the offer.

The alarm produced by Havelock's success drew the leaders together again, and the troops, instructed by the Moulvie, submitted to their authority, but refused to proceed beyond the Alum Bagh, till a large sum of money was distributed among them; when they marched out, in great pomp, to leave their guns and shoes to the English at Oonas, Busheerutgunj, and Nawabgunj, to which they ventured to return only when well assured that the "Ironsides" were not there, but across the sacred waters of the Ganges.

The mischievous ascendancy of the Moulvie over the troops began more and more to endanger the courtiers, who struggled in vain to humble the presumptuous fanatic. He had somehow gained a high reputation for courage, of which the authorities of the Palace were utterly destitute; and, by working on the religious credulity of the troops, and encouraging their excesses, he became the hero of the army, which believed in his invulnerability, even after a bullet from a British rifle had smashed his thumb. The conceit and bombast of the fellow were peculiarly pleasing to Asiatics, who consider it the essence of authority to assume the airs of greatness, and to affect to be under the protection of the Gods.

The inaction of Havelock, for awhile, greatly raised the spirit of the runaways, who entreated to be led on to Cawnpoor, and only desisted on its being explained to them, that, though hitherto favoured with victory, they might fail in so desperate an undertaking, when it would be easy for the defenders of the Residency to effect their escape. The great Commanders, exhorted by the Begum, harrassed the Europeans in the Residency; and, as far as arranging for their destruction, made most desperate efforts; but the troops had been so often repulsed, and were so convinced that the whole of the defences were undermined, that neither threats, rewards, nor reproaches, could get them on to the walls again. They had a wonderful opinion of our proficiency underground, and it was the current belief that we had subterranean passages to the granaries of friends in the city, through which we replenished our stores; and the report caused several grain merchants to be closely watched, and forbidden to go to market for more!

The Court of Lucknow, anxious for encouragement from the Emperor, despatched a special envoy to Delhi loaded with presents, which were received without any particular mark of condescension; and, after staying several days to observe the desperate and disheartening posture of affairs in that doomed city, the envoy returned to Lucknow with letters overflowing with joy at the extirpation of the infidels, and a mouth full of lying stories of the marvellous valour of the mutineers within, and the deplorable condition of the British troops outside the stone fortifications of Delhi. Letters of congratulation were afterwards exchanged, and their arrival at Lucknow was always announced by Royal salutes, and dancing and singing in the city; the noise of which reached the Residency defenders, without exciting more than intense curiosity to know the cause of so much gladness. The last Imperial missive was followed by a messenger from the Ganges with intelligence that Havelock was building a bridge of boats, and a few days later that he was crossing into Oudh; which suddenly stopped the fiddlers and dancers, and threw the whole city into a panic. Councils met and dispersed without fixing on any plan of resistance, and leaders swore to the courage and fidelity of their troops without going out to prove it. The hour of trial brought discord and dissension among the Chiefs, and shameful reproaches from the Begum, which only produced the customary amount of oaths to vanquish the cursed infidel, or die in attempting it. Rajah Man Singh, up to this time, had kept his force of guns and matchlock-men away from the rebel camp, and given the Chiefs no more than his hearty good wishes; but now he joined the bewildered Council, and restored its confidence by offering to go himself and beat back the impudent invaders.

The citizens were warned, by proclamations, that the English would surely convert them to Christianity if victorious, and exhorted, in the name of God, to cooperate in defending the religion of their fathers. They were reminded of the massacres at Cawnpoor and elsewhere, and assured that the English would avenge them, in Lucknow, by the indiscriminate slaughter of women and children; and they were told that the infidel army was so small that it must be defeated if courageously opposed. The mass of citizens remained at home, and made their preparations for leaving the city, knowing pretty well, from experience, to which side the hand of victory pointed. Mutineers and matchlock-men from the province, after tying up their valuables to be handy for flight, proceeded to the Alum Bagh in the wake of Mummoo Khan, the paramour, who was dragged there in a ricketty carriage-and-four.

Outram and Havelock again crossed the Ganges, unencumbered by baggage, and rapidly advanced, through torrents of rain, to cut their way to the little garrison of Lucknow. A short fight won the Alum Bagh, and the following morning, after an obstinate resistance, the enemy were driven from the masonry bridge leading into the city. The prodigious mass of undisciplined and disheartened rebels fell back upon the palaces and mansions skirting the river, creating the utmost alarm. The Begum and ladies of the Kaisur Bagh, fearing for their lives, implored to be allowed to leave the city, from which thousands were already in full flight. Shurf-ood-dowlah, the Prime Minister, aware that little more was needed to drive the whole of the troops away, stopped them, and, placing himself at the head of a band of volunteers, issued from the Palace to oppose Sir James Outram and Havelock as they approached the Red Gate. A shell bursting among them threw the whole gang into disorder, and the minister was carried back, groaning, with a disabled arm, for which he afterwards got very great praise.

Some Europeans, Christians, and friendly natives, (amounting to about thirty,) captured in Lucknow, and sent in from the Province, were retained in prison, where they endured hunger and insult more horrible than death. After the defeat at the Alum Bagh, a mutineer regiment, encouraged by the Moulvie, demanded the surrender of the prisoners, who, enclosed in a rope, were led outside the Kaisur Bagh and slaughtered, the women being exposed naked to the ribaldry of the executioners. The troops were led to commit this atrocious deed by a suspicion that the courtiers would secure their own safety through the English captives, and afterwards betray them; and, by murdering the prisoners, they hoped to compromise them to an unpardonable degree.

The British leaders reached the Residency, and, dreading to pursue their success too far, with their reduced force, remained there; and, in a few days, the camp of the mutineers rang with cries of victory, which fetched back the host of cowards that quitted the city, to re-enact, for nearly two months more, with few variations, the farce already described. The Moulvie's reputation for valour reached so great a height that he boasted of being an Incarnation of the Deity, and the folks of the Palace found it difficult to prevent his usurping the entire control of affairs. His predictions of complete success; of the ultimate extension of the rule of the army to the sea; and of "beating his drum in London," flattered the misguided wretches, and hurried them on to repeated assaults on the new positions occupied by General Outram, from which many never returned. The mutineers were increased by fugitives from Delhi, who, however, were held in small estimation by the Oudians, and kept at a distance, in order that they might have no pretext for sharing in the booty of the Residency.

The advance of Sir Colin Campbell, for the final relief of the beleaguered garrison, was prepared for in a more orderly manner than before, after the troops had extorted more money; but his fiery progress quickly produced a panic, which lasted till the withdrawal of the heroic defenders of Lucknow, and the retreat of the English; a movement the rebels viewed with surprise, and celebrated by rejoicings. Before the termination of the siege, they buried upwards of ten thousand men!

CHAPTER XVI.

Sir James Outram at the Alum Bagh—Great rejoicing at the departure of the Heroes of Lucknow—An Army of Donkies led into danger by a King of Monkeys—Sir Colin Campbell's host—Journey from Calcutta with a gentle jeweller and a cunning gold digger—The great William Howard Russell and his wicked mare—Sir Hugh Rose did well—Siege of Lucknow—Ordered to be shot for going over to the enemy—A dangerous development disliked by Adrian Hope—Sir James Outram across the river—The Martiniere captured—The gallant Anson—Jung Buhadoor and his odoriferous Goorkhas—Begum's Palace captured—Captain Macbean's eleven heads—A terrible storm in the Kaisur Bagh—My good guide Kunoujee Lal.

WHEN the garrison was withdrawn from Lucknow, it was proposed to abandon the province of Oudh for the present; but, at the earnest request of Sir James Outram, he was allowed to brave, on a plain outside the Alum Bagh, the whole of the insurgent army—nearly tenfold greater than his own. It was a bold venture, for the country all round was supposed to be hostile, and he had a communication of nearly fifty miles to preserve with Cawnpoor.

The enemy for awhile spent time in rejoicing at the forcible ejection of the Residency defenders, for no one dared say we had defeated and out-manœuvred them for fear of being killed as a liar and a coward. Many took home their plunder and their boastful tongues to excite the avarice and martial ardour of their benighted neighbours, who saluted the braggards as I would have bowed to our greatest captain. In the city the notes and noises of revelry resounded in the mansions of the mighty men of a little Court; and the common soldier, and professed vagabond, impudently vaunted his valour, and overawed the humble citizens by his ferocity. Monster processions fearlessly marched up and down the broadest streets, filling the air with brazen sounds and the roll of great and little drums, and noisy chants that sent the English to perdition and exalted themselves to paradise. Generals and nobles went out, with great glasses, to look derisively at the heroic little force which was to be exterminated on the conclusion of the feats of victory; and rode home again to curb the fiery spirit of their followers, who could scarce brook the delay, so forward had they grown out of danger.

Sir James Outram calmly waited for the onslaught, caring very little how, or when it came. His troops settled in canvas homes, and enjoyed the fine English sports of quoits, racing, cricketting and betting, hoping that the fun would be increased in the morning by a general action. At last the rejoicings were over—the enemy came out—looked—and went back again, bearing a few imprudent men home on litters. The same thing was performed, with trifling variations, till the enemy, prompted by the Gods, hit upon an expedient which had been successful, before the Christian Era, in the cause of King Rama, of Ajoodia, in Oudh. The sovereign of Ceylon—so old are the triumphs of beauty!—smitten by the charms of Queen Seeta, forcibly carried her from the house of Rama, who was driven from his kingdom. His efforts to recover the lovely Seeta were unsuccessful, till he invoked the aid of the monkeys, who, under their leader Hunooman, built a bridge over the ocean, across which the avenging army passed into the ravisher's citadel, and recovered the sorrowing damsel.

Now no one in Oudh is impious enough to doubt Rama, Seeta, or the Bridge across the Ocean; and although Monkies have degenerated to monkeys, Hunooman is a fact, and Hunooman may be personified. The martial host of Oudh, on a fine morning, covered the plain and threatened to encircle the camp of the impudent foreigner; and, if the British General had not been previously informed of the artifice, he might have been surprised to see Hunooman, after a lapse of twenty centuries, again at the head of an avenging army. There he was, tail and all, waving a sword far in advance of his force; which, happening to be composed of reasonable beings, did not advance too far, and before long Hunooman disclosed his humanity by lying down to die, and his followers their discretion by leaving him alone to do it.

Sir Colin Campbell, meanwhile, had dissipated the Gwalior army, and swept the miscreants of Furruckabad from the town polluted by innocent blood. Men and material were gathered at Cawnpoor for the complete capture of Lucknow, and the re-occupation of the province of Oudh; and the public impatiently waited for the advance of the Commander-in-Chief, who at last started—with twenty thousand troops, forty thousand followers, and fourteen miles of baggage!

The Government having *dismissed me from the Service* after the relief of Lucknow, I was at liberty to follow my own inclinations, and I chose to rejoin Sir Colin Campbell. I was anxious to share in the capture of a city which the courage and devotion of my comrades had rendered famous, and I hoped to be useful again during the progress of the army through the narrrow streets and the numerous handsome palaces of Lucknow. I travelled up from Calcutta with a gentleman whose jewels were going to the Governor-General, at Allahabad, to bedizen the faithful; and with another who was proceeding, hot haste, to Bithoor, to lead a forlorn hope to forty million pounds sterling, concealed by the progenitors of the Nana. Whether the men who wear the jewels were faithful, or whether the earth surrendered its enormous riches, I have not heard. At Cawnpoor I learnt that the army had been two days gone; and, without waiting for servants or baggage, I started in the company of Captain Trevor Wheler, of the 1st Bengal Fusileers, who was the owner of a poor little nag which we could easily have carried between us. He alternately carried us; and, as the night was dark, the road dangerous, and we alone, he had little rest till we overtook a detachment of the Rifle Brigade, under the command of Captain Thynne, a handsome and gallant gentleman who was afterwards killed. As we neared our resting place for the night, Colonel Macpherson, Quarter Master General of the Army, mounted on a dromedary, went jogging and jingling by, hastening to join his Chief, who took care to have the best of officers with him.

The following morning we reached the army, and as I passed the tent of the lively, clever, and enterprising Captain Patrick Stewart, he invited me in, and introduced me to a gentleman whose portly form was incased in a semi-military suit, and his smiling face shaded by a wide-awake suitable for the crown of a Special Correspondent. I stood before the renowned man, unawed by his look, which would not have frightened a child, and unabashed by his erudition, which was familiarly employed to provoke good humour. I, so humble and so small an individual, actually grasped the hand which had sent tingling, to the hearts of Englishmen, the griefs, the joys, and the triumphs of the Crimean Army; whose pen had made and unmade, and who was now present to record the deeds of the dwellers in the canvas houses spread drenching around us. The dark heavy clouds that had screened us from the sun during our march, had just let go their contents, and the whole camp was soon afloat.

Mr. William Howard Russell, L.L.D., is a very wicked man, for the very next morning he let me mount a mare which had pitched him, all against his will, to the bottom of a great trench, and nearly buried him for good. The beast was unmanageable, and would not walk excepting when she chose, and then the motion was like a lively strathspey. After passing the camp of Sir James Outram, I turned her head back to go there, and it was only by the intervention of Providence that I was not carried over to the enemy, who watched me from their cover a mile off. She was brought to a stand only by running her against one of the redoubts constructed for the security of the outposts by Sir James Outram. Never ride the horse of a Commander-in-Chief, or the mare of a Special Correspondent of *The Times*.

While the drama was being enacted our side of India, Sir Hugh Rose, with singular dash and daring, had made prodigious marches, indifferently supplied by everything but courage and endurance. With signal success he proceeded, under a scorching sun, through central India, pursuing the enemy to their strongholds, and forcing them one after the other in spite of numbers and obstinacy. He always overtook an enemy to chastise him, and when the history of his campaign is condensed, it will bear comparison with the best of the operations for the suppression of mutiny and rebellion.

When the Residency was abandoned I was decked in a red tunic, stitched by a lady of the garrison; French-grey breeches, once worn by a noble fellow lying in the ruined churchyard; a felt helmet, belonging to the Commander-in-Chief; and coarse jack boots. Now I presented myself to His Excellency in the handsome uniform of the Calcutta Volunteer Cavalry Guards, which I joined after the volunteers had given up all hope of an insurrection. Sir Colin smiled at the well-dressed trooper as he bent before him in shining cavalry boots, reflecting everything but the wearer's conceit. He was as strong, hardy, and determined as before, but now possessed an army which could have gone, *without its baggage*, all the way to the Caspian. The eye far south encountered tents, carts, and cattle, lodged on hills and in dales, which sent clouds of dust to choke the swarming scarlet host, who impatiently waited for the famed army of Goorkhas to participate in the assault.

The force was at last put in motion, and the enemy learnt what it was to be behind defences that let in showers of shot and shell, and let out themselves. Mounted on a great chesnut horse I inspected the rifle pits of the insurgents, and ventured so close, that by a miracle I escaped from their malice nearly to be deliberately shot as a deserter by order of an English officer. This happened on our left, and I next rode across the river on our right to "develope" the fire of the enemy, who lay hid in high fields. I slowly rode down their front, accepting every bullet, to the annoyance of Brigadier Adrian Hope, who expected to be forced to expose his men to fetch in my body. I had joined the army to be useful, and gratuitously ventured to feel the enemy in a direction Sir James Outram was to go the following morning. I may here remind the reader that I am a civilian; and, being under no military control, could almost go wherever I liked. No other civilian, however, would perhaps have been suffered to do so much, and I have to thank my military friends for the good humour with which they viewed my forwardness, and accepted my services.

Sir James crossed the Goompty by a pontoon bridge; manœuvred to the village of Chinut; and drove the enemy back to their lines, where the 2nd Dragoon Guards imprudently followed, and dropped their intrepid leader, Major Percy Smith. I remained with Sir James, acting as his aide-de-camp, till the close of the engagement, when Captain Oliver Jones* and myself rode back to the Head Quarters with an escort. At the request of Sir Colin I went in the night with the heavy guns, after resting for a couple of hours on the damp banks of the river, wrapped up in the cloak of Colonel Riddell, R.A. I returned alone in the afternoon with a note from Sir James to the Chief, riding in a straight line between the two camps, past the defences of the enemy, who yelled and sent a few shots after me. As

* This gallant naval officer went to India to witness the glorious exertions of his countrymen to extinguish the flames of the Mutiny; and he was always prominent, as a volunteer, whenever they were engaged with the enemy, who wounded him once in a hand-to-hand encounter.

I crossed the pontoon bridge the Highlanders were rushing upon the enemy in the Martiniere, and I only reached them in time to see Brigadier Adrian Hope withdraw his Highlanders from the park, through which shot and grape poured from the high defences lining the opposite bank of the canal.

Early in the morning I again joined the force across the Goompty as it formed up in the bed of a stream, and followed the 1st Bengal Fusileers, and 79th Highlanders, who impetuously pursued the insurgents with deadly effect, and pressed forward, in the general advance along the left bank of the river, through villages, gardens, and standing crops, till Sir James stopped at the Badshah-i-Bagh, and turned his artillery upon the extensive and massive fortifications covering the Palaces. I had often before noticed the hardihood of the Hon. Captain Anson, on the staff of Brigadier Sir Hope Grant, but this day, as he fearlessly rode through woods and lanes, far in advance of the skirmishers, I trembled for his safety. He is an excellent swordsman, and cared very little for numbers as he pushed through them, followed by Captain Moorsom, on the staff of Sir James Outram—a kindred spirit whose ardent and intelligent soul left us soon after.* At the close of the day's proceedings I returned to the camp of the Commander-in-Chief, fatigued, and glad to repose awhile away from the din of war.

At last Jung Bahadoor, G.C.B., arrived, with the famed and stinking army of Goorkhas, to co-operate in the assault: they were preceded by the reputation of

* Captain Moorsom accompanied Havelock's force for the relief of Lucknow, and his knowledge of the city, and daring spirit, made him one of the best officers with it.

their wondrous deeds. Sir Colin saw them—embraced the renowned Hill Chief—the Scotch pipers rejoiced at the meeting—British and Nepaulese guns roared the glad tidings abroad—and, the giant Hope Johnson suddenly heightened the effect, by stepping hot and excited through the crowd to announce the capture of the Begum's Palace. The enemy, cut off from retreat, met with the fate of the defenders of the Secunder Bagh, and more than five hundred burning and mangled bodies covered the area, through which Colonel Leith Hay, of the 93rd Highalnders, and Captain F. Middleton, on the staff of Sir Edward Lugard, carried spears dripping with blood. I hastened to the Palace, where the fight was finishing in a corner house, close to which Captain Macbean, of the 93rd, had just lopped off eleven heads, as they turned their eyes to look for him. He declared "he did na mean to hurt 'em!" and, under his muscular arm, they must indeed have died without pain. A regiment of Goorkhas was *pushed* up to join in the assault, but they only took part in the plunder, to the disgust of the Highlanders, some of whom endeavoured to quicken their movements by threatening to shoot them.

Lord Clyde now occupied the whole of the outer line of defences, which the enemy had constructed, at great trouble and expense, with the avowed intention of defending them—if possible. Sir James Outram and Lord Clyde, in concert, day and night bombarded the intervening squares and the Kaisur Bagh, and poured such a storm of shot and shell upon them that many deserted to the west end of the city, where the citizens were already sufficiently alarmed by the mere noise of the cannonading. The plan of the Commander-in-Chief was to drive the enemy from each position by his artillery, and assault only when the guns failed to disturb them. The army of Jung Bahadoor, was allowed to stay on the left, where the Goorkhas supposed they had the post of honour, because the enemy almost let them alone, and they picked up a few abandoned guns and bundles of old rags. These conceited little creatures went on duty with very great pomp, and left it, strongly scented, with very great joy. They beat more drums and blew more trumpets in their camp than Lord Clyde did in his; and boasted to each other that they were doing all the work.

My good guide, Kunoujee Lal, was employed again in the intelligence department; and the plans in the hands of the Chief of the defences of the enemy, were prepared on information brought out by him after visiting the several places. He had remained with Sir James Outram at the Alum Bagh, and, before the arrival of Sir Colin Campbell, repeatedly visited the enemy as a spy. He was most useful, and, there can be no harm in repeating that—he was *badly* rewarded.

CHAPTER XVII.

aval guns and Lieutenant Young—A woman's appeal of no avail—Assault led by Captain Da Costa—Da Costa killed—Imprompta seizure of the Kaisur Bagh—British pluck under a steam engine—A Christian captive released—My plunder—The Palace sacked—The famed Residency captured—Reflections therein—Horse wounded—A frightened family saved from drowning—Captured an English gun—Sack of the City begun—Mrs. Orr and Miss Jackson rescued—Captain F. Middleton and Lord Clinton are shown some "fun"—Sir James Outram disapproved of the sport--The Moulvie attacked by, and escaped from, Sir Edward Lugard—Murder of the Prime Minister—The last fight for the City.

THE naval brigade, under the command of Captain Vaughan, brought their heavy guns to bear on the temporary defences surrounding the large Mausoleum of he father of the Ex-King of Oudh; and Lieutenant Young, who carries an enormous heart in a little body, beat in an opening, which the enemy took small pains to prevent. Their second line of defences were massively built of earth, on the scarf of a great ditch, mounted by numerous guns, and occupied by a multitude of mutineers. But the poor men were exposed to the incessant explosion of large shells from both sides of the river, and dreaded that there was a diabolical plan to surround them and prevent their retreat. They were so disheartened that the enraged and disappointed Begum in vain appealed to them for some evidence of their boasted prowess, and at last, in despair, taunted them by an offer of breeches, which are worn in India by the gentle instead of the hardy sex. The Council that previously wanted the treasure guarded by the defenders of the Residency, assembled in great trepidation, and sent forth long proclamations inviting soldiers and citizens to co-operate in the extermination of the infidels, who, (praises to the Holy Prophet!) were daily diminishing, and all but vanquished, as manifested by the heads paraded in the city. The Council had no faith in their own statements, nor had anyone else; on the contrary, the more they boasted, the more the fear of the people increased.

When the breach was practicable a storming party of Siekhs, under the command of Captain Da Costa, of the Indian army, was brought forward, and I accompanied it as a guide. The enemy abandoned the Mausoleum as soon as we mounted the breach, and Captain Da Costa pursued them through the large archways of the enclosure, and, turning to the left, continued at a run, exposed to a heavy musketry and random artillery fire, till he reached the fortifications of the Kaisur Bagh Palace, where he was stopped by a deep and broad ditch. He was brave and impetuous to excess, and his fine handsome face was lit up by that noble flame that burns so strong in British officers. His fiery spirit had already carried him too far, and he was ordering his twenty Siekhs to attempt to cross the ditch into the Palace defences, when I ventured to point out that it would be a useless sacrifice of life. He had advanced so fast that the storming party was not together, and the reserves far behind.

"Who are you, sir! to interfere in my duty?" The gallant fellow did not know who I was.

"I do not wish to interfere, and am only here as a guide, willing to obey and follow you. Reflect whether it is prudent, with twenty men, to go unsupported into the midst of at least five thousand mutineers. Kavanagh is my name, which you may have heard before."

Da Costa seized my hand, and, while warmly pressing it, expressed a willingness "to be guided by one already renowned as a guide."* We then withdrew to a building known as "The Printing Press" to fire into a crowd of mutineers who were deserting the fortifications in our rear and on our right. His daring soul was excited again, and he would have rushed on the multitude of runaways had he not been stopped by a wound in the stomach which killed him during the day! This officer had joined the force as a volunteer, only a few days, and, at his earnest entreaty, he was attached to Brasyer's regiment of Siekhs.

Brigadier Russell shortly after advanced with the reserves, and occupied the magnificent buildings overlooking the Palace defences, from which the rifles of the 90th Foot quickly dislodged the enemy. Brasyer's Siekhs were again pushed forward with some of the 10th Foot, and, almost without opposition, entered the north quadrangle of the Palace in pursuit of the enemy, who abandoned all the fortifications towards the river. Some of them were surprised in the Steam Engine House by Captains Radcliffe and Francis, of the 20th Foot, who greatly distinguished themselves, and covered the enclosure with the bodies of three hundred mutineers.

I suggested to Brigadiers Russell and Franks that the

* This little incident gave me so much pleasure that I venture to mention it at the risk of being thought conceited.

Palace be forced by a passage known to me; and, to show its feasibility, I mounted to the roof of the shops in the street, and climbed over the parapet of the Palace walls. Captain Sir Henry Havelock came next, and, while he surveyed the proposed passage, a gun, a short distance on our right, attempted to disturb him. The assault soon followed, and the Siekhs and 10th Foot entered the Palace this side, while the 90th Foot forced an entry eastward. The advance was so rapid that before Sir Colin Campbell was aware that the first assault under Da Costa had succeeded, the British arms were fusilading the mutineers within the finest square of of the famed Palace. I followed the Siekhs into the principal building, and carried one of its large green silk window-curtains to the highest turret to shake at the enemy, who resented my audacity by trying to shoot me.

The tidings of the impromptu capture of the Kaisur Bagh brought on large reinforcements with the Commander-in-Chief, and he quickly occupied all the fortifications of the enemy, who made great haste out where nobody detained them. Firing, fighting, plundering, and the destruction of valuable property, continued all day, the enemy obstinately defending only one square of the Palace, till the Queens and grandees retreated under cover of darkness. At the request of Sir Robert Napier, I accompanied Colonel Harness round the squares, to dislodge the enemy concealed in the chambers; and, in one of them, I found manacled a fair Christian drummer-boy, who had been ten months in captivity. I sent him to Sir James Outram, who has generously retained the lad in his service ever since.

The enemy artfully left loose powder in several

burning buildings, that exploded and did damage to our troops, who incautiously ventured everywhere in search of plunder. On this occasion I picked up a silver mug, worth about six pounds, to work into a pretty memento recording the fact of my having been the first person to enter the Palace, and I took away the rich cover of the seat of a silver throne. The throne itself was pulled to pieces by the Sickhs before I was done flourishing the green curtain over their heads. I afterwards gave the cover to Lord Clinton, of the Naval Brigade, and the mug is lost. This was all I ever plundered, notwithstanding that very few of the assailants had as many chances of enriching themselves. Glory, not plunder, was my ambition: both seldom go together, for they are separate and antagonistic passions.

It was amusing to see the gallant fellows so eager for the fight in the morning, disguised by large protuberances all round their bodies, produced by the spoil. Some carried clocks, vases, trunks, pictures, and silver maces—others trailed rich silk quilts after them—many bound their heads and waists with gay shawls and satins—a few were completely clothed in Oriental Court dresses. The European soldier usually snatched up one article and was off; but the Siekh perseveringly tried every door, every box, every bundle, and every floor, and only ceased when gold and silver rewarded his exertions. The confusion and uproar in the chambers was very much heightened when thousands of camp followers pressed in to go again over the ransacked rooms, and add to the destruction of property too heavy to carry away. The licence of plunder has an injurious effect upon discipline, and reduces officers to the level of soldiers; but it is a right sanctioned by long usage, and is so consonant with the avarice of man, that it can never be entirely stopped, either by Provosts, or Prize Agents.

Sir Robert Napier and Colonel Harness examined the approaches to the Residency, and Sir James Outram came from the other bank of the river to conduct the operations for the entire dispersion of the enemy from the city. There were no more fortifications to be forced, but it was possible that the troops would be engaged in the streets, and arrangements were made for this by providing the assaulting columns with guides acquainted with the city. I was sent with a detachment of the 23rd Royal Welsh Fusileers, under the command of Major Bruce, who entered the Baillie Guard Gate at a run, and pursued the mutineers into the city towards the Cawnpoor Road.

Once more I stood in the building where I had dwelt throughout the siege of 1857, and, as we lunched on the floor, I gave utterance to the feelings excited by the past. Those five months of trial had not been without joy, and the recollection of that unequal struggle will always be pleasant to all but the mourners. Here I had suffered sickness and want—been harrassed by real and feigned attacks—had escaped from death by a miracle, for I always courted danger—mourned for the loss of good friends carried off in their prime, and endured unusual anxiety for the safety of my family. Here, too, I had seized the only chance ever presented of establishing a fair character for courage and devotion among so many devoted and courageous comrades; and it was from this spot that I had ventured on the enterprize which won the admiration of my countrymen.

When the defenders retired from the Residency it

bore evident marks of the desperate character of the siege: many of the buildings were falling from the effects of the enemy's shot, and all were more or less dilapidated. Now, most of the houses were level to the ground, and the rest were in a ruinous condition. The rebels had begun clearing the spot to build a "Market of Victory," so that the fame of their prowess in expelling the Infidels might descend to the end of time!

I joined the advanced column in the afternoon, and at the request of Sir James Outram, conducted through the Muchee Bhawun Castle, the 1st Bengal Fusileers, who, led by Major Salisbury, drove the enemy beyond the great Imambara. I next proceeded up the Chouk, or main street, (through which I had passed on the night of my escape,) with a party of the 20th Foot, the enemy retiring down the streets as we approached. My horse was wounded in the shoulder while riding by the side of Captain Carnegie, the City Magistrate. The citizens precipitately abandoned their homes, leaving all they possessed behind. I ventured thrice among them, in advance of the troops, to dispel their fears, but they would not stay, and I narrowly escaped being shot by armed men concealed in the crowd. The rebel leaders had industriously circulated a rumour that the English intended to sack the city and destroy the inhabitants; and, as none of the enemy had ever escaped from us, and great licence had been permitted, the rumour was believed. Some families taken by surprise threw themselves into wells, and Major Carnegie and myself had the gratification of drawing up three females and a man from one which we reached in time to save them.

A fire of small arms was maintained all night on both

sides, and in the morning we continued stationary, being contented for the present with the possession of nearly two-thirds of the city. With a Serjeant's party of the 20th Foot I reconnoitered the streets in advance, to ascertain how far off the fears of the rebels had carried them, and during the search discovered a party gathered round an English nine-pounder brass gun. By a sudden rush we drove the gunners away, and brought it in to our lines.

The sack of the city now began, and when I returned to the same place the following day, (after witnessing the capture of the Moosah Bagh, far on our right, and the occupation of the mansion of the Prime Minister, Shurf-ood-dowlah,) every house was literally turned inside out. A spectacle of ruin and wilful destruction of property presented itself everywhere. The mansions of the rich were ransacked over and over again, and the humble goods of the poor were thrown into the street, and the floors dug up for their earnings. How sad for the unfortunate wretches who dared not stay to guard them!

The Goorkhas, finding that the enemy had retired from their front, pushed through the city and joined their advanced post with ours, after Lieutenants Bogle and McNeil had gallantly rescued Mrs. Patrick Orr and Miss Madeline Jackson from the house of Darogah Wijid Ali, who has since been rewarded by the grant of ten thousand pounds for preserving the two ladies from the massacre that deprived one of a husband, and the other of a brother.

The following afternoon I was starting with six Goorkhas to reconnoitre the west of the city when Captain Frederick Middleton, A.D.C. to Sir Edward

Lugard, and Lord Clinton, of the *Shannon*, came to me with the hope of seeing some "fun." We proceeded about a mile beyond our posts unopposed, and forced our way into a large temple. Middleton and Clinton pursued some of the enemy round the inner building while I was engaged in a room with three swordsmen. I was so fortunate as to disable the first by a blow on the head, which broke my sword in two; the second, thinking me powerless, made a desperate cut at my neck; but I happily dealt him one across the face that rolled him on the floor. The third turned about. I pursued and stunned him by a blow on the head; and, as he fell, I stumbled forward in a gateway, and was instantly run over by several of the enemy, who were so frightened by Middleton's desperate onslaught that they did not see me! The Goorkhas looked on, and it was not their valour that saved us.

We were suddenly checked in our adventurous career by loud voices calling to each other to go on; and, as we were not altogether without discretion, we turned homewards. The Goorkhas attempted to run off as the noise increased and occasional shots wizzed through them; but, as our safety existed in showing a bold front and in retiring as if strong in numbers, Middleton and myself held our fists in their faces, and made them check the enemy, who, luckily for us, were no better than themselves. We were uneasy about the spirited young nobleman, and to get him out of danger sent him back for reinforcements.

Two hours afterwards we returned with sixty Goorkhas and three of their officers, thinking that Sir James Outram would approve of the occupation of the Temple, as so much ground gained for the column which was next morning to attack the Moulvie Ahmud-oola, who was strongly posted in another large temple in the neighbourhood. The enemy slowly retired before us because we made little progress with the Goorkhas, who flew into every open door, and waited to be shamed out by Middleton and myself. They fired over the houses with wretched old muskets that took some seconds to go off, and then kicked violently. The officers were worthless, and the soldiers were of such bad stuff that they bodily rushed on the wounded as if they had only come out to go back with the first man hit. At last the Temple was reached and occupied. The enemy disappeared from the neighbourhood, and the Goorkhas were earnestly instructed to stay there till morning. Sir James Outram, however, disapproved of placing a force there, supposing it would alarm the Moulvie and cause him to retire from his position in the city, where there was a good chance of killing or capturing the miscreant. Had the Goorkhas not come home of their own accord long before midnight, perhaps their close proximity might have frightened Ahmud-oola and his gallant company, for among them the mountaineers had a prodigious reputation for valor.

With unaccountable pertinacity the Moulvie continued to stay in the city after the enemy had been driven from every position but the sacred Temple of Huzrut Abbas. He had the character of being brave, and his present attitude was one of defiance. Sir Edward Lugard advanced against him in the morning, and was so unfortunate in his arrangements, that the whole column was drawn into a long narrow street, and bore onward without knowing whither they went.

Major F. Middleton and myself, assisted by four Siekhs, endeavoured to discover the cause of a commotion on our left flank, and suddenly came on the enemy in a large square, apparently preparing for retreat. We killed some, and Middleton was on the point of being shot by a Sepoy, whom he mistook for one of our Siekhs, when I undeceived him, and the mutineer fell dead by a bullet from his revolver. Before intelligence from us could reach Sir Edward some of the troops in the street were mowed down by grape from a couple of guns at point blank range, and the pressure backwards almost amounted to a panic. The column paused, and fired at men behind walls, who threw down bricks from the roofs of the houses. The noise and confusion was very great. A few of the houses were forced by the Siekhs and Highlanders, and from one of them I discovered a passage from the street into the Temple. Middleton, always thirsting for honour and glory, was again in front, and assisted by a Highland pioneer, we broke through two doors, and were beating at a third, when we heard sword cuts and the screams of women within the Temple. The thought occurred to us that the wretches were murdering their women! The blows at the strong door increased in force, the screams touching the heart of the generous Highlander; and, when it yielded to the hatchet, six of the 93rd, Middleton, and myself, pushed through the opening. The defenders who had not gone off with the Moulvie were shot, sabred, or bayonetted, and we found on the floor the warm but lifeless body of Shurf-ood-dowlah, the Prime Minister of the rebel government. He was suspected of corresponding with the English, and, refusing to buy his safety, was barbarously murdered by order of the Moulvie as he quitted the Temple; and it was this bloody deed that provoked the screams of the women.

This was the last fight for the city, and, by desire of Sir James Outram, I resumed my civil duties, to check plunder and other excesses, and to encourage the return of the citizens to their forsaken homes.

CHAPTER XVIII.

Ancient and modern Oudh—The City deserted—The Goorkhas carried away all the rags—Citizens returned and were plundered—Fell from the top of a house—Streets cleared of the dead—Talookdars of Oudh—General Walpole buried Adrian Hope at Rohya—An awful fall down a well—Another fall from a dog-cart—Belief in a a good destiny useful—Nawab Mosim-ood-dowlah, uncle of the Ex-King of Oudh—New fortifications, and the demolition of the City—Greedy Prize Agents—Colonel Abbott and his embellishments—Administrative Reforms by Sir Robert Montgomery and Mr. George Campbell—Sir Hope Grant at Nawabgunj—Volunteered to go over to the enemy to explain the pacific intentions of Government.

THE province of Oudh has occupied an important position from the earliest ages, and its people were renowned as warriors and scholars long before Europeans emerged from darkness. It was once an extensive kingdom, and its rulers, who boasted of their descent from the sun and moon, have furnished heroes and heroines that figure conspicuously in the mythology of the Hindoos. The devout still make long pilgrimages to their shrines at the ancient capital of Ajoodia. When the empire spread to distant parts, the kings removed to Kunonj, where they reigned in peace, and encouraged those arts and sciences which are now the only study of the Pundits. The Hindoos were a steady, industrious, and intelligent people, and, in contented and prosperous homes, made laws and minded them, till the fanatic

Mahomedan descended with his broad scimitar to spread dissention and voluptuousness, to devastate the provinces of the Hindoo princes, and to substitute a rotten empire of his own. The gorgeous and venerated capital of Oudh afterwards rapidly dwindled, and, in the twelfth century, its ruler was killed, its riches plundered, and its palaces and mansions reduced to ruins.

The Mahomedans erected a capital at Fyzabad, near the ruins of the ancient city of Ajoodia; conquered neighbouring states; and, under a Khoorasam merchant, (who founded the dynasty of Oudh,) attained a high position as a tributary of the Emperors of Delhi. Successive rulers enlarged their authority, and at last they ventured to oppose the arms of the clever and victorious Lord Clive, who greatly curtailed their dominions. The Maharata soldiery had overrun and occupied the province of Rohilcund. The Ruler of Oudh was invited to expel them for four millions of pounds, and when their ejection was accomplished, the Rohillas would not pay. British aid was purchased to compel them, but the Oudh prince in his turn pleaded inability to pay. Finally, he surrendered to the English the provinces south of the Ganges, and reserved to himself the fertile territory known as the Province of Oudh. He was raised to the dignity of king, and swore to administer just and equitable laws, and to restore peace and prosperity to his turbulent little dominion.

The capital was a third time changed from Fyzabad to Lucknow; and, in the course of half a century, it became famous for its size, its elegance, and its infamy, in the midst of misrule without, and debauchery within. The extravagance of the kings attracted idle and dissolute crowds to Lucknow, and, in spite of lax laws and corrupt governors, it grew rich in commerce and gorgeous palaces. Every year added to its wealth and its dimensions, and the Court of Oudh was soon regarded by the people of the East as the abode of learning and illustrious kings. Enfeebled by the excesses of the harem; surrounded by infamous fiddlers, dancers, and drummers; and deceived by corrupt and dishonest courtiers, the king withdrew from the business of State, and ultimately shut himself up in the gardens of the Palace. Here he contentedly passed his time in writing good verses, composing figures for dancing, and chasing, in the guise of Cupid, the angels of his seraglio. The engagement to administer justice was more and more disregarded, and, if it had not been for the presence of English troops and English officers, the whole of Oudh would have been overrun by bandits and stranglers. Warning after warning with difficulty reached the ears of the king; and, when there was no prospect of improvement, the country was reluctantly annexed to the British dominions, and occupied without a single attempt at opposition.

The city covered an area of twelve miles, and its inhabitants were roughly reckoned at more than half a million. As our battalions pushed through the city in pursuit of the enemy the people precipitately retired, and, when I resumed my civil duties, it was almost empty! Only camp followers and soldiers traversed the streets, (which smelt strongly of the dead,) plundering deserted houses, and savagely destroying everything too heavy to remove. The Goorkhas carried even rags from the street, and it was only the want of carriage that prevented their taking away the very bricks of the buildings.

By long and frequent marches into the surrounding country with detachments of the 93rd Highlanders I succeeded in dispelling the fears of the citizens, and in persuading thousands to return to their pillaged homes. Many of the aged and feeble died of misery and want, and the city was filled with lamentations for the death of their relatives, and for the loss of jewels and treasure hoarded by years of industry. The distress was greatly increased by gangs of camp fellows that stopped returning citizens and deprived them of the little saved when escaping.

Armed bands from our irregular native regiments persisted in breaking into houses, and in robbing, violating, and sometimes murdering the unfortunate wretches whom I had brought back. The officers appointed to restore order to the city had no rest, and for several days the drummers of the 93rd Highlanders flogged marauders from the camps. The officers felt much compassion for the miserable inhabitants, and spared no pains to protect them. On one occasion I chased into a large house some of Hodson's Horse, (who gave great trouble,) and followed the ringleader to the roof. He leaped into a yard twenty feet below, and in attempting to catch him, my scabbard tripped me, and I fell over the parapet and was stunned.

The inhabitants seeing we were in earnest, and encouraged by us, combined at last to protect their homes, and after a fortnight they ceased to be molested. We then obtained time to remove the dead from the trenches and sewers, into which they had been dragged, and to clear the streets of the filth accumulated during the nine months reign of the rebel government.

Sir Colin Campbell followed the enemy only a few

miles from Lucknow; and the mutineers, after running in hot haste to remote places, and greatly alarming the rebel hosts abroad, ostentatiously marched back to take up positions with the impudent hope of checking any attempt of ours to disturb their reign of terror trans-Gogra, where they thought we would not follow them.

Several of the Oudh chiefs sent in their submission and offers of assistance after the fall of Lucknow, but withdrew them as soon as it was known that the British troops were hutting themselves for the season, and showing but few signs of vitality. Many indeed were powerless, till we could protect them from the vengeance of the mutineers and from those Talookdars who were provoked by our cruel policy before the war. The splendid Brigade of Highlanders and Siekhs quitted Lucknow for Bareilly, and at the small and unfinished Fort of Rohya, it was the misfortune of the General to leave many of them dead in a ditch. He then proceeded onwards, with a force depressed by the loss of the good, the gallant, and the noble Adrian Hope, and other devoted officers and soldiers.

Several regiments of infantry, and some artillery, stayed in the palaces and temples of Lucknow, while the cavalry remained in the groves without. I first occupied a Mahomedan shrine at the west end, and so peaceful were the citizens that I was for some time alone, away from any troops. The fall from the house still gave me pain, when I was invited to dine at the Mess of H.M. 20th Foot. Hurriedly proceeding after dusk to the Mess Room in the Chutter Munzil Palace, (still like Murad the unlucky,) I fell heavily to the bottom of a well leading to the lower cellars. Loud groans brought me help, and I was lifted to the top, and lay all night in the General Hospital in great agony. Though I fell on to a brick floor, by the mercy of Providence, I escaped a second time with a whole body. The skill and care of Dr. Grant, of H.M.'s 53rd Foot, (one of the most able and amiable surgeons in the service) sufficiently restored me, at the end of a fortnight, to venture into the city, in a dog-cart, with Captain Wilkins, of the 7th Hussars, (who was wounded in the foot and hobbled about on crutches,) and a minister, who was recovering from fever.

We passed up the route followed the night of my escape to the camp of Sir Colin Campbell, and while I was eagerly recounting, and they listening, to my exciting story, the horse stumbled and fell. In an instant the face of the minister grew long with fear, as he desperately clutched the back of the cart, with his legs in the air; Wilkins flew off, taking his sticks with him; and I lay under the body of the horse, too helpless to extricate myself, or to turn my face from the legs of the animal, who made desperate efforts to paw himself out of the broken shafts and harness. I expected my face would be kicked, and roared for help, which was at last afforded by a native who, jumping from his stall, seized my arms, and dragged me out of danger. This mishap confined me again, and my friends talked of a cat with nine lives, because I escaped so many dangers without serious damage. Before this narrative closes, you will be inclined, reader, to say with them, that seldom has it been the fate of any to encounter so many perils with so little injury. I began to think that the Almighty had protected me for some purpose; and, as it is a useful and a happy conceit, I mean to make no effort to dissipate it, but go to on working as if it were a fact. Who knows!

Lucknow soon became the most disagreeable residence in the world. The heat of the weather increased, and the perpetual marching and counter-marching of troops, with provoking lines of baggage, dug up the dust which the hot winds of the season sent flying up and down the roads to our great discomfort. Gradually we sheltered ourselves in the houses of the city, and gathered a few odd articles of furniture from deserted or confiscated mansions. I settled in a house belonging to Monuwur-ood-dowlah, the uncle of the Ex-King of Oudh, a nobleman with a decided preference for the English. His costly mansions were plundered by the enemy while he remained concealed in the country waiting for an opportunity to seek our protection. His known partiality for the foreigner lost him all influence; and his retainers deserted him at the commencement of the war.

We had scarce got rid of the marching troops and their baggage, when the Engineers, under the indefatigable Sir Robert Napier and Colonel Crommelin, began those imposing fortifications that now overlook and ornament Lucknow. The finest portion of the city was levelled to the ground by thousands of naked natives, who daily perched on the tops of the houses, and worked with pick-axes, while hundreds of pounds of powder were exploded to assist them: producing altogether the delusion that the work of demolition was being executed by demons. This unavoidable work of destruction still further distressed and impoverished the inhabitants, and the operations of the Prize Agents nearly completed the sack of the city, for they mercilessly sprang at every morsel of treasure discovered through the informers, and were not particular as to whether the owners were rebels or no.

To these misfortunes the people resigned themselves as only Orientals can do, and took shelter away from the demolitions, where they hoped to be left undisturbed. After a time they detected a thin line suspended over their new abodes, and flags at equal distances; and this they shortly learnt was a notice to quit, as way was wanted for three new roads a hundred and fifty feet broad, and for the range of the great guns mounted on the fortifications. The unlucky wretches sorrowfully resigned themselves to the worst, and were afterwards not surprised by the multitudinous visits of officials for war-taxes, house-taxes, rents, registries, and I know not what else. Do not be angry, reader, for such things are unavoidable in India. The people are very wicked and foolish, and do not know as well as their governors what is good for them. If the army mutinies the people must be plundered, and the Government must build forts. If the cleanliness of civilization is to be introduced, way must be made for wind, and sewers for water; and who .ut the people should pay for it?

As soon as order was restored to the city, and the streets cleaned, useful reforms were introduced, and extraordinary efforts made to replenish the treasury by revenue collections from the neighbouring villages, and by seductive applications to distant landholders, some of whom actually came into Lucknow with their arrears of rent, to find their houses burnt, their fields destroyed, and their lives threatened on their return home. The Commissioner, Colonel S. A. Abbott, devoted much attention to the embellishment of the east end of the city, and he everywhere improved the communication by the construction of roads and bridges.

Sir Robert Montgomery, who succeeded Sir James

Outram after the capture, has great administrative experience, and it was applied to effect reforms that were much needed. Previous to the mutiny the proceedings of our civil courts were recorded in the vernacular language; and, as most officers could not read it, and many had no leisure to go through the volumnious depositions and orders put before them for signature, it gave rise to abuses and to the most ruinous delay. The procedure was simplified by Mr. George Campbell, the able Judicial Commissioner of Oudh, and perfected by requiring European officers to examine the parties of a case themselves, and to record their evidence in English; which at once secured what was wanted—a quick, and an impartial record, by an honest official. The change was approved by the people, who have cenfidence only in European officers. The same procedure was extended to the criminal courts, and the punitive laws modified so as to exclude petty offenders from our jails, which used to be needlessly crowded under a system by no means reformatory.

During the month of July, the temerity of the enemy induced Sir Hope Grant to proceed to the east with a small force, with which he defeated a large body of the enemy twenty miles from Lucknow, at Nawabgunj. An expedition to the south had previously gone out, and came back, under an awful sun, followed by Benee Madho's cavalry, who put it abroad that they had beat us in, and got great praise for the lie. Our troops were really vanquished by the heat, which killed a great number of the infantry.

Attempts were made by letters to induce the rebel chiefs to return to their allegiance, and some did withdraw from the unequal contest, and others promised to do so on an opportunity offering. The successes of the British army in the other provinces had so disheartened mutineers and rebels that they began to fear for their very existence, and now fought in despair. Some of us thought that much of their obstinacy proceeded from a disbelief in our professions of forgiveness, which only reached the rebel army through doubtful sources; and there was reason to think that the war might last TOO LONG. The hostility of the people was not general because they were unconscious of their power, and it was only the absence of unanimity arrested that knowledge. The possession of it would have aggravated our difficulties tenfold; and a protracted struggle, if it did not disclose their strength, would at least still more unsettle society, and spread a passion for disorder and violence to distant and undisturbed provinces. Moreover the state of Europe seemed to forbode a war there before the contest in India could terminate.

There never was a strife in which the belligerents were so entirely cut off from each other. The enemy feared to approach us, because we either imprisoned or destroyed all who fell into our hands; and, although we had to contend with the ignorant, to whom the enlightened should be indulgent, we made no suitable effort to appease their fears or win their confidence, besides sending letters to a few who dared not openly acknowledge them. Government had no intention of pursuing a war of extermination. On the contrary, Lord Canning was humane to an extent that was condemned then, but will be appreciated when the passions provoked by the cruel events of the mutiny have subsided.

It seemed to me that a messenger of peace, acquainted

with the people, and bold in his office, could remove much of the doubt that kept them aloof, and that the presence of an accredited English officer would be at attended with beneficial results. The feeling which led me to pass through the enemy in disguise to help ourselves, now prompted me to go openly among them to endeavour to put an end to a merciless war that was devastating our own territories, and ruining more innocent than guilty men. Late in June, 1858, I volunteered to go over to the rebel leaders with a flag of truce, but my superiors would not avail themselves of the offer, and the unnatural struggle went on as before.

CHAPTER XIX.

The City—Ordered to Muliabad—Troops without ammunition—An angry officer—Police posted at Ruheemabad and surrounded by the enemy—Attacked and defeated by Lieutenant Ffrench—Police rewarded for gallant defence—A brave native collector—The enemy frightened by a road—Agriculture unaffected by the war—Landholders assembled for sports at Ruheemabad—Talookdars backward—Policy to Talookdars reversed—People should be taxed—Oudh Military Police—Town of Sundeela attacked by Captain Dawson—Prince Feroze Shah, of Delhi, with 600 cavalry, defeated by fifty Siekhs.

THE demolitions continued, and the city rapidly assumed a clean and prosperous appearance. Most of the citizens returned, and some of the leading men of the rebellion accepted the pardon offered to them, and endeavoured to settle down in their quiet homes. The road to Cawnpoor was protected by troops at Bunnee and Nawabgunj, to the south; and Sir Hope Grant's force to the east guarded that side of Lucknow. To the north our territory extended only a few miles, and westward it was secured at the extremity by untried Irregular troops that made no effort to check the encroachments of the enemy, who presumptuously threatened to besiege them at Muliabad.

The Chief Commissioner, Sir Robert Montgomery, in a very encouraging note from his Secretary, requested I would proceed to Muliabad, and endeavour to extend our influence further into the district of Mullaon. I reached the garrison in the afternoon, and learnt that there was not enough ammunition to defend the place twenty-four hours! I expressed surprise to Captain Dawson, and he was displeased with me for doing so. He had about fifty native cavalry, five hundred infantry, and no guns: while the enemy had fifteen hundred infantry, two hundred cavalry, and three guns. Reports reached during the day that they meant to attack us, and another arrived, while we were at dinner, informing us of their advance. I again pointed out to Captain Dawson how embarrassing it would be to send troops from Lucknow to relieve us, supposing the want of ammunition did not oblige him to abandon the post: which exasperated him so much that he lost his temper, and the public service seemed likely to suffer by his intemperance. His generous temper, however, returned the following morning, when he admitted the oversight, and at once obtained an ample supply of ammunition. He consented to a proposal to attack the enemy, some of whom had come as close as Ruheemabad. They retired as we entered the village, and I posted a party of police, under two Head-men inimical to the rebels, who were joined by a few villagers, which raised the party to about forty armed men. We visited the villages in the neighbourhood to warn them against assisting the rebels should they attack the police who were hastily located in a house indifferently fortified.

Early the next day reports followed quickly of the advance of the rebels to Ruheemabad with two thousand men, and four guns; and, in reply, I desired the Head-men to stay at their post and defend it till relieved. They waited to be surrounded; refused to surrender;

and manfully resisted frequent attempts to carry the place by assault. Lieutenant Ffrench, of the 53rd Foot, Adjutant of the Police, and myself, started to their relief with forty cavalry and five hundred infantry, and on nearing the place I found matchlock-men of neighbouring villages resisting the attempts of the enemy to pass towards Muliabad. The rebel infantry, under cover of high reeds and garden plants, fired on Lieutenant Ffrench as he impetuously descended a high mound and engaged them. I kept his right flank secure from cavalry till the rebels began to retreat, when I advanced at a gallop, and fell upon a large body of matchlock-men as they issued from the village in full flight. After doing good service my sword snapped on the shield of a tall swordsman, and my horse was wounded as I rode him down. The main body of the enemy flew off under cover of a ravine. Lieutenant Ffrench, reinforced by the rescued garrison, in vain endeavoured to overtake them, they ran so very fast. With our cavalry we afterwards scoured the country around, and warned the owners of villages to co-operate in the defence of the police; which they were willing enough to do where we could save them from the vengeance of the rebels.

The beleaguered garrison had a few men killed and wounded, and behaved so well, against great odds, that Sir Robert Montgomery consented to reward them with money grants, as an encouragement to others; and I gave each a written statement of his gallant service. The Tuhseeldar, or native revenue collector, who followed me into the midst of the enemy, was brave to rashness, and during the combat he alone engaged several swordsmen, for which I presented him with a Colt's revolver. The Siekh cavalry fearlessly dashed into the crowd, and with their sharp swords greatly quickened the speed of the runaways, who ran nine miles off to their head quarters in the town of Sundeela.

By desire of the Chief Commissioner I constructed a road to Lucknow, to facilitate the passage of guns, should it be determined to add a European force to the native troops with Captain Dawson. The rapid completion of the road so alarmed the enemy, that they increased in numbers at Sundeela, and threatened to march on our fortified position at Muliabad before we could be reinforced. We took no notice of the boast, and every day made long patrols to within a short distance of them, and even drove in their cavalry picquets.

The rebellion had nowhere interrupted the industry of the agriculturist, whose summer crops, moistened by the rains, now covered the face of the country with a beautiful green mantle, which was rent here and there by numerous groves of tall umbrageous trees bearing the luscious fruit of the season. Through these flourishing fields, and under a terrific sun, we rode to reassure the landholders, and draw them into a meeting at Ruheemabad, where I purposed amusing them with sports and compromising them with the enemy. There was a fair assemblage of landed proprietors, who came to the gathering with matchlocks, and heartily joined in the sports of the day. But the Talookdars pleaded illness and kept away, for their sympathies were decidedly with the enemy, whom they secretly encouraged to oppose us. These men, at the annexation of Oudh in 1856, were deprived of their villages, and the small proprietors on their estates encouraged to harrass them by suits in our courts. The official bias was so strong against the whole body of Talookdars, that every pretext was seized to lessen their property and to degrade their position. Every deed of infamy committed before the annexation was attributed to them, and almost every acre of land in their possession was supposed to have been acquired either by force or by fraud. With singular imprudence we revived old claims, and disturbed landlords many years in possession.

That harsh policy, which was merited only in a few cases, was now reversed. Talookdars were restored to all they had lost, and many proprietors whom our regular courts had reinstated, were summarily turned out wondering at our inconsistency. The disclosures of the war had exposed our folly in this and in many other things, and the Government seized the earliest opportunity of amending the errors of the past. The Barons, or Talookdars of Oudh, are generally idle, sensual, and uneducated; but under a generous system of administration they will doubtless improve before the close of the century. European officers can exercise a most beneficial influence over them *if they have leisure to do it.* No system of administration can be perfected with an imperfect establishment of officers, and until this defect is remedied, the Home Government may order, and the Local Government threaten, without increasing the quality as well as the quantity of work done. If it were only to add to the number of administrators the taxes proposed by Mr. Wilson ought to be imposed.

After the capture of Lucknow in March, 1858, a force of military police was organized for civil duties. The cavalry regiments were largely recruited from the Punjaub, and the infantry was composed of Siekhs, and men of every shade of religion: experience having taught that it was better to mingle the castes and disregard the prejudices so greatly pampered before. The cavalry with Captain Dawson was formed of Siekhs and Affghans, and the infantry of Siekhs, Pasees, and other low caste men. Most of them had never been under fire prior to the little battle of Ruheemabad, where they were very forward in engaging the enemy.

The enemy grew bold, and began to replenish their treasury by plundering villages supposed to be friendly to us or backward in assisting them with armed men. The supplies of the city of Lucknow, moreover, were checked by the position of the rebels at Sundeela. Captain Dawson, therefore, consented to go on to Sundeela, sixteen miles west from Muliabad, to capture that important town, which was reported to be occupied by fifteen hundred infantry, two hundred cavalry, and five guns.

The time seemed favourable for attacking them, for the spirited progress of Sir Hope Grant towards Fyzabad and Sultanpoor had somewhat disheartened the rebels throughout the province. Our troops on the Cawnpoor road were also threatening Prince Feroze Shah on our left, and a rumour was circulating that the dreaded Highlanders were crossing the Ganges into the district.

On the afternoon of the 10th of August Captain Dawson advanced with a small force to Ruheemabad, where we were joined by two small Talookdars, some of the native gentlemen of Sundeela and Muliabad, and Chowdry Hushmut Ali, a handsome man, with considerable influence, who abandoned the cause of the rebels on the final occupation of Lucknow. They were accompanied by about four hundred matchlock-men on whose valor we could not depend. In the evening we rode, with a small escort of cavalry, to within five miles of Sundeela, and I sent a watchman of one of their own villages to warn the leaders that we would attack them in the morning, and be disappointed if they again ran away. A native is half beaten when you frighten him, and I was sure that the message would cause them to make early arrangements for retreat before they thought of defending the town.

It rained during the night. The morning was cool, and the country around rich in ripening crops of wheat. We started at dawn, and crossing a rapid stream by an old stone bridge, passed under the shade of a mangoe-grove with its delicious fruit, on to an extensive plain studded with brush-wood, and covered by the rain of the night. Midway to Sundeela we halted for breakfast, with the cavalry of the enemy watching in our front and on our right flank. Before we finished our repast a letter was delivered from Bharut Singh, (a good loyal Baron residing beyond Sundeela,) informing us that the enemy, in consequence of my message to the Chiefs, had been reinforced during the night, and now had six hundred cavalry under Prince Feroze Shah, three thousand regular and irregular infantry, under the notorious Chiefs Namdar Khan and Gholab Singh, and five guns, one of which he described as large.

This was startling news, and it caused us to discuss seriously whether we should proceed further with only fifty cavalry, and five hundred infantry, and *no guns.* The native chiefs were of opinion that we were too few, and frankly advised us not to rely on their followers. Hushmut Ali was the only one who concurred with us in thinking that there were only so many more to run away. From a mound we surveyed, through our glasses, large bodies of cavalry and infantry standing under extensive woods screening the town in our front. Captain Dawson arranged to attack them to the south, and thus avoid the fire of the guns mounted on an earthwork commanding the high road. He made over the gallant troop of Sowars to me, and with them I covered his advance from the rebel cavalry, who retired to the south, and assembled in columns of troops with the intention of sweeping down upon my handful of horsemen. I put on a bold front, and sent them further back, by a feigned charge, to secure Dawson a passage into the suburbs of the town, where a rapid discharge of small arms and cannon checked him for a few minutes.

The six hundred cavalry led by Feroze Shah drew closer, and their steady advance was so menacing that I was forced to decide at once between attacking them or going into the town. The first would have disheartened our infantry, who were already engaged at great odds, and I, therefore, invited the Siekhs to say whether they would follow me. With one accord they lifted their swords, and called to me to go on. Feroze Shah drew nearer, but, as I turned to engage him, he halted on the edge of a large grove of trees, apparently uncertain what to do. I again asked the troop whether they would do it, as we went on as if to engage their centre, and received the same response. In another minute we suddenly turned from the straight line, and were engaged hand to hand with the left flank, which broke at once, and threw the whole body into such confusion, that they turned about and went away, pursued by the Siekhs.

Followed by a dozen Siekhs, I started after the Prince,

who was conspicuous from riding a grey horse and being dressed in white. We became so mixed with the retreating cavalry, and in such peril from the difficulty of telling one from another, that he distanced us, and the desperate efforts made to cut our way through were stopped after a few minutes by a shot which disabled my horse and threw me to the ground. One of the enemy, passing at a gallop, struck at me while down: I threw up the hilt of my sword, and was slightly cut on the hand. A second cut through the heel of the left boot, and slightly wounded me. Another stopped so suddenly to reach me that his horse fell on his haunches, and I was enabled to seize him by the neck and drag him from his seat as the animal recovered itself. I spared him as a mark of respect to the cavalry, for he was a fine young Sikh who had deserted from the Residency during the siege of Lucknow. They were, however, greatly exasperated at his treachery, and while I was pursuing the enemy on another horse, he was sabred, and left for dead on the field.

We disabled about forty of the irregular cavalry, who were so well mounted that a couple of minutes stoppage enabled them to get out of sight behind the woods and villages north of Sundeela. From thence they went hot haste, eight miles off, to the fort of Birrwa, to which place the infantry and three little guns were following them when I reached the rear of the town to hasten their movements.

CHAPTER XX.

Captain Dawson's assault on the City—Spirited conduct of Military Police—An Irishman's honour proved by surrendering to the enemy—The leader's charger captured—A loyal Talookdar hastens the retreat of Prince Feroze Shah—Chowdry Hushmut Ali left in Sundeela with 700 matchlock-men—Return to Muliabad—Thanks for our victory—Revenue settlements—Dawson reinforced—Troops remove to Sundeela—A hasty assault repulsed—Wounded in two places—Bharut Singh Talookdar—Removed to Lucknow—Dawson besieged in Sundeela—Relieved by Brigadier Sir George Barker, who gained a signal victory.

CAPTAIN DAWSON was resisted in the streets as he endeavoured to push on to the main body defending the guns. Stones, bricks, and earthen pans were flung from the roofs on to the heads of his men, who eventually discovered an outlet, and pressed forward to the right, led by the native Adjutant and Soobudar Ram Singh, while Dawson engaged them on the left. The matchlock-men were of no use except to cover his rear, where they crowded together in a fright after the first discharge of grape. The steady and spirited conduct of the Military Police at last overcame all opposition, and, as the enemy attempted to carry off their best gun, the gallant Ram Singh rushed through a lane, and in capturing it received two severe wounds which disabled him.* Dawson fell

* This excellent officer was sent into Lucknow for medical treatment, and mysteriously disappeared from the hospital before he had recovered. He was with Sir Hugh Wheeler at Cawnpoor during the siege, and escaped with a letter from him to Sir Henry Lawrence, who promoted him for his gallantry.

upon a large party defending a garden and compelled all to retire but twenty-five, who threw themselves into a large masonry house surrounded by a brick enclosure, and obstinately resisted the efforts of the Siekhs to bring away the tumbril of the gun from under their fire. Another large house was carried by assault, and the town cleared of the enemy who had been some time flying towards the Fort of Birrwa, when I engaged their rear.

I afterwards rejoined Captain Dawson in the town, and found him urging his Siekhs to bring in the tumbril, near which three of his men had already been killed. I suggested that it would be better to put his men under cover, and leave the rebels and mutineers in the house till we refreshed ourselves, for there was now no occasion to expose his fine fellows, who were jabbering away in great joy at the success. The attention of the enemy was, in the meantime, withdrawn from the tumbril by feigning to make a mine under a corner of the house on the opposite side; and, on our return, they were so completely occupied watching the proceedings there, that we succeeded in removing the tumbril to the side of the captured gun, from which I sent two chain shots through the door of the upper room filled by the rebels. Dawson wanted to take the house by a rush; but he must have suffered severely, and as the battle was won, it would have been a needless sacrifice of life. They maintained a deadly fire on the doors leading into the yard. From the side of one of the doors I summonsed them to surrender, which they refused to do, declaring that it was better to die fighting than yield to a foe who would hang them.

"I will spare your lives." I spoke from under cover.

"We do not believe you! Who have you spared to-day? Have you not hitherto killed or imprisoned all who ever fell into your hands?"

"I cannot offer you free pardon, but I swear that you shall not be killed if you surrender. You cannot escape, and we could soon overcome you."

"We would surrender if we believed you," one of them replied.

I could think of no other way of assuring them. Divesting myself of my arms, and pulling the Siekhs back from the passage, I walked from under cover into the centre of the yard, and placed my life at their mercy.

"Now do you believe me?"

Three of the defenders had been killed. The others at once threw down their arms and fell at my feet! The Siekh soldiers, however, clamoured for their blood, and I had much difficulty in preserving their lives, for Dawson, not liking what I had done, kept aloof till his better feelings returned, when the uproar was subdued and the prisoners properly cared for.

During the forenoon I captured the white charger of the leader Namdar Khan, but the animal was so wild and difficult to manage that I afterwards gave him away. Bharut Singh, the loyal Talookdar, joined us as soon as he saw the enemy on the wing homewards, and he greatly accelerated the speed of Prince Feroze Shah, as he accidentally crossed the fire of his two guns. Captain Dawson and myself rode out to the neighbouring villages to encourage the people back to their homes, for our victory was incomplete while the town was empty of its inhabitants. The defeat of the rebel army, by so small a force, gained us great renown in the country, and alarmed the malcontents far off. Formal letters of congratulation poured in from Talookdars, and offers of men and money—the mere effects of fear, which I took pains to increase by threats of attacking them if the enemy were let return to Sundeela during my absence.

Chowdry Hushmut Ali had extensive property in the town, which the rebels levelled to the ground for his desertion to the English. But his influence among the peasantry was undiminished, and our victory now gave him sufficient authority to induce him to hold the place with his own men, and with assistance from Bharut Singh, and other Talookdars. We slept at Sundeela, and in the morning started back to Muliabad, the villagers on our road turning out to look at the little force that had vanquished so many of the enemy, and were taking home their largest gun. The sensation everywhere was considerable, and we took advantage of it to reinforce Hushmut Ali, and to invite the villagers to keep him there till we made other arrangements for securing our conquest. At Ruheemabad the police post was strengthened by the addition of a company of Siekhs, and workmen were engaged to complete a fortification bagan some time before. As we left for Muliabad the guns of Bharut Singh were heard announcing that the assistance promised by an important Talookdar had reached Hushmut Ali, who was able to report to me, in a couple of days, that he had seven hundred matchlock-men and seven Talookdars by his side.

Sir Robert Montgomery and my immediate superior, Colonel Barrow, were delighted at the success of the Military Police, and the Governor-General thanked us for our gallantry. The most forward of the cavalry and infantry were selected for promotion by the Chief of

Police, and so excellent a spirit was infused into these raw levies, that Captain Dawson was now ready to attempt anything with them.

Long rides in the sun and rain began to affect my health, and I was glad that this victory enabled me to repose for awhile, and attend to civil duties which the extension of territory had increased. Disputes of every kind were filed, involving troublesome enquiries; and small landholders came from distant places hoping that their early submission would exclude the recusant Talookdars from the settlement. Many, with no right whatever, obtained engagements, pretending to be the owners of villages not in their possession, and these were afterwards greatly disappointed because we ignored them. The war had stopped all petty crimes in towns and villages, and our Courts were closed for the present against civil suits. I hope to be excused for stating here that I never hung, or, (excepting in fair fight,) never shot a "nigger," and I rejoice that the resentment roused by the cruelty of some of the enemy, never provoked me to revenge it on men only guilty of resisting the foreigner. Many executions were justified by the emergencies of the time, but many more resulted from intemperance, notwithstanding the efforts made by Lord Canning and others, to stop indiscriminate slaughter. His Lordship is doubtless not ashamed to be called "Clemency Canning."

On the 21st of August Dawson was reinforced by a regiment of Police Infantry commanded by Capt. Graham, (one of the gallant defenders of the Residency,) and a regiment of Police Cavalry, under Captain Melvill, with Lieut. Hawkins as its Adjutant. Lieut. Ffrench, of H.M. 53rd Foot, was Dawson's Adjutant, and Dr.

Cape was Surgeon of the whole force. With so many English officers we had the presumption to think that the Military Police could be led through the whole Province; and, as we marched on to garrison Sundeela, extravagant schemes of conquest were laughingly discussed. We were welcomed into the town by a salute from the guns of the Talookdars, whose followers, in their picturesque robes, looked on from high mounds and houses lining our route to an immense grove of lofty trees, under which we pitched our tents. The town of Sundeela is beautifully wooded, and the country around was then luxuriant in the crops of the season. It rained incessantly, and the floors of our canvas homes were often buried in pools of water. Our arrival drew in many luke-warm landholders, and, at a parade of the auxiliaries,we counted over a thousand armed men who professed a willingness to go on to the fort of Birrwa.

The cavalry patrolled daily towards that fort, and once went round it under fire of the guns of the enemy, who had no horse to oppose them, for Prince Feroze Shah got so bad a character by his flight from fifty Siekhs, that he went twenty miles further off to other friends. On the the evening of the 24th of August Captain Dawson decided upon reconnoitering Birrwa with a force of five hundred infantry and three hundred cavalry, but, when he started the following morning, I learnt that it was his intention to attempt the capture of the fort, of which neither of us knew anything whatever! I ordered the native Chiefs to follow quickly with their two guns and their matchlock-men, and in vain recommended that ladders and hand grenades should be taken on.

Nearly all the villages on our route were deserted, and the guides were so terrified that they led us astray through high and wet fields of cultivation, and only recovered themselves as we neared the first fortified post of the enemy, which was precipitately abandoned by everybody but an idiot, who was—shot! From the walls of the fort, which was built of mud on a high mound overlooking the country, we saw the long outer defences of Birrwa: the inner works being completely concealed by graceful bamboo trees with their branches closely entwined. To the east, west, and north, the defences were hidden altogether by the same plant, which grew close up to the walls, and seemed to be impenetrable. The ramparts of the south front were crowded with armed men, and some of the enemy loitered in a hamlet below us, till Captain Melvill advanced with his cavalry, and drove them into the fort. Under cover of the brushwood the infantry approached and stopped on the plain facing the south line.

I again ventured to urge that the assault be delayed till the native Chiefs arrived with their men and guns, when they could be usefully employed in diverting the attention of some of the enemy to the west. But Dawson despised them, and at once advanced against the fort, from which a rapid fire of guns and matchlocks were directed against him. I succeeded in drawing him, from the whole of the front fire, to the west angle, where he was able to form up his men, under cover, within a few yards of the walls. The native officers here asked to be led to the assault by me, and Dawson readily consenting, they followed me to the nearest bastion, from which we dislodged the enemy. With only fourteen men it was impossible to cross the ditch which was twelve feet broad, and fourteen feet deep. But the suddeness of the assault drove the enemy from the breastwork overlooking us, and none of them would return till they observed me unsupported by the main body, which lingered in the jungle. My comrades now begun to fall, and I was myself only saved by the devotion of two Siekhs, who threw themselves before me, and were killed. I sent back a Siekh to urge on the reserve, and, as he left, a bullet struck the revolver in my belt, and threw me down. I rose and was then slightly wounded in the shoulder as I pointed to the loop-holes before us to frighten the enemy, who did not perceive that my pistol was unloaded. There was still time to benefit by the position I had gained, but no one advanced from the jungle, and I was again wounded by a bullet which passed into the right shoulder, and splintered the top of the bone. The gallant fellows with me were killed or disabled, and I was alone for half-a-minute, when some Siekhs and Hindoostanees rushed to my assistance, followed by Captain Dawson, who went back for support on my offering to hold my ground. My wounds bled profusely, and in another minute my companions were all disabled. I was now weak and helpless, and with difficulty staggered back to the jungle, pursued by the fire and yells of the rebels, and protected by a miracle. Captain Dawson, supported by his spirited Adjutant, Lieut. Ffrench, attempted to force the defences, but the right moment for action was missed, and he was repulsed with the loss of many gallant men.

To attempt to capture one of the strongest forts in

Oudh without ladders and without guns was presumptuous; but it was not impracticable, for the two defeats of the enemy at Ruheemabad and Sundeela had greatly disheartened them, and, if the first assault had been followed up, the place would have been abandoned. The native Chiefs reached us after the repulse, and, carried in a sedan, I employed their two guns, and matchlock-men, to check any impudent attempt to pursue us while the wounded were cared for, and the police rested under the shade of the trees at a distance. Captain Melvill, with his cavalry, cut up some of the rebels who flew from the fort at the first attack, and he prevented reinforcements reaching them from a neighbouring Talookdar. My wounds were bound up with a wet cloth, and in the evening the police force returned to Sundeela.

I posted Bharut Singh, Talookdar, in the fortification abandoned by the rebels on our advance, and with three hundred of his followers, and two guns, he subsequently prevented their taking any advantage of our mishap. Dr. Cape skilfully extracted the bullet from my shoulder, and I endeavoured to discharge my office duties; but the pain increased, and I became so weak, that Captain Alexander Orr had to be sent out to relieve me and I was carried into Lucknow, where I was attended by the civil surgeon, Dr. Douglas.

A month after my departure a force of about twenty thousand rebels, with guns and cavalry, crossed the river Goompty—the Military Police did nothing to stop them—and they were soon surrounded and besieged in the town of Sundeela. The infantry, under the command of Captain Dawson, with Graham, Ffrench, and Dr. Cape, successfully resisted the efforts of the enemy to reach the large buildings in which they were entrenched; and, when Sir George Barker arrived, two days after, with a small force, (composed of the Rifle Brigade of the 2nd Battalion, the 38th and 88th Foot, and two squadrons of the 2nd Dragoon Guards,) the police sallied out, and assisted to clear the town, which the rebels gave up with little opposition.

The enemy stopped at a village five miles off, and prepared to defend an admirable position on a mound with low brush-wood protecting their flanks. The following afternoon Sir George Barker attacked them. The police carried the right; the cavalry drove back the left; and the European infantry broke in upon the centre and captured the guns. The 2nd Dragoon Guards, commanded by the dashing Colonel Seymour, and the Police Cavalry, led by Captains Graham and Chamberlain, and Lieutenant Hawkins, followed the enemy for several miles; and, before the pursuit closed, over fourteen hundred of the enemy encumbered the line of retreat, among carts, cattle, litters, tumbrils, and loose baggage abandoned in their great haste to get away.

CHAPTER XXI.

Engineer Hospitality—Banquet to commemorate the Relief of Lucknow by Outram and Havelock—Col. Bulwer going to the war—Fort of Seelimpoor surprised by Bulwer, and Simon Martin—The people unfriendly—The monster Munsub Ali—The courage of a loyal native severely tried—His revenge at Seelimpoor—A hot ride through neutral ground—Night incursions of the enemy—Return to Lucknow to meet my family—Benee Madho, and Colonel Bulwer's three victories—Ordered to Sundeela—Forts dismantled, and Chiefs humbled—An old man, with an old retrospect.

The engineers were quartered in a splendid mansion adjoining the Kaisur Bagh Palace, and they dispensed their hospitality in a style that might be expected where such frank and cheerful spirits as Major Teddy Oakes presided. On the morning of the 25th September, 1858, a party of the defenders of Lucknow assembled there for the purpose of celebrating the anniversary of the reinforcement of the garrison by Outram and Havelock. The story of the siege was recounted in laudatory speeches; the "heroes," absent and present, were adequately praised; a silent toast was drank to the memory of the noble fellows who died in the unequal struggle; and the good things on the table were more and more inflaming the generous feelings within us, when we were suddenly drawn outside by the laughing voices of a detachment of troops marching out of Lucknow to attack the enemy.

It was a lovely night, with the moon and the stars shining and sparkling as is only to be seen in the beautiful blue autumn sky of the East; and the Comet, which afterwards attained such great proportions, was then lifting its head and waving its prodigious tail in the eyes of the enemy, who regarded it as presaging famine and an increase of the calamities of war. The infantry, mounted for the first time in their lives on miserable ponies and donkies with and without bits to guide them, passed by in grotesque groups, kicking and thumping little beasts, that anon pitched their riders, and ran through the crowd of laughing equestrians, disturbing their seats, or left the noisy medley to draw breath, and pick up a stray straw on the road side. The men enjoyed the novelty of this queer ride to the contest, and their merry voices could be heard long after they left our sight.

The following morning we heard the thundering noise of Colonel Bulwer's artillery, and, during the day, we learnt that he had surprised the rebels in the fort of Seelimpoor; had carried it by assault, inflicting great damage; and chased the enemy into the river Goompty: which engulphed a large number of them, and increased the casualties to about seven hundred. His detachment was composed of a wing of that splendid regiment the 23rd Royal Welsh Fusileers, two guns of the Royal Artillery, and a regiment of the Oudh Military Police. Mr. Simon Martin, of the Civil Service, (one of the most amiable of the defenders of Lucknow,) accompanied the force, and, with some native police, did good service in clearing the fortress. That officer held the important appointment of Deputy Commissioner of Lucknow, and the heavy and responsible duties of his office rendered it necessary that he should return to the city at once. As European troops could not be left without a civil officer, on whom the commander was dependent for information of the rebels, and for some of his provisions, I was directed by Sir Robert Montgomery to join Colonel E. G. Bulwer, if well enough to do so. My wound had partly healed, and I was beginning to regain strength. Tired of the dull life my confinement enforced, I was glad of the opportunity of returning to the field, and, the next morning, my tent was pitched, beside the gallant Colonel's, at Goosaingunj, twenty miles east of Lucknow: to which village he retired after the capture of Selimpoor.

Here I found the people more hostile than in the west of Oudh, owing to the presumptuous bearing of Benee Madho, who paraded the country with over twenty thousand of the hardiest men in the province, and threatened death and destruction to all friends of the cursed Furingee. Munsub Ali, (a cruel upstart who was denied his estates on the annexation for plundering and oppressing his neighbours,) carried out the menace on the bodies of all persons suspected of corresponding with the English. It was to destroy the mischievous power of this wretch that Seelimpoor was captured; but the dread of his brother remained, and the people kept aloof, excepting in our immediate neighbourhood, where they were sure of protection. The crimes perpetrated by the monster were sufficient to deter the most loyal subject, for he sometimes disemboweled his victims, and I once heard of his loading an unfortunate scribe with powder, and firing him off as if he were a piece of ordnance! He was among the rebels drowned in the river Goompty in attempting to escape from the avenging arm of Bulwer; but a brother succeeded in crossing the stream who had been an active promoter of Munsub Ali's diabolical policy, and he endeavoured to organize a force to arrest our further progress, encouraged by Benee Madho, who promised to fall on us by-and-bye.

By long and frequent excursions into the country we deterred them from attempting to molest our small force on the heights of Goosaingunj, where I began the restoration of an old fort, in which a body of police were nearly annihilated a short time before. A native, who had gone through the siege of Lucknow, was promoted for his loyalty; and, several miles away from any support, and almost without ammunition, was posted in this dilapidated fort, with about fifty policemen, in the hope of his being let alone to collect some revenue from the villages around. Munsub Ali surrounded him: a sham fight was maintained all day, which exhausted the Thanadar's ammunition: a wretched little gun on one of the bastions burst itself, after terrifying the enemy by its noise. At night the strings of the gate were forced, when some of the defenders escaped through the darkness over the walls, while the Thanadar, followed by the rest, mixed, unperceived, with the assailants, as the crowd of screaming wretches pressed in; and, in a very short time, he reported, *in propria persona*, the defence and disaster to his superior at Lucknow. This lucky man, after escaping two great sieges, was sent with the force of Colonel Bulwer; and, at the back of Mr. Simon Martin, he revenged himself on the bodies of the creatures in Selimpoor. He was a good, honest, servant, and I engaged him on the work of restoring the defences, although he made no secret of his dislike to being caught behind them again.

On the left, between Nawabgunj-Burabunkee, on the road to Fyzabad, and our own position at Goosaingunj, there was about twenty miles of country unoccupied by us, and seldom frequented by the enemy. I thought we might as well show ourselves in this neutral ground to restore the feeling of ownership, and to drive in the landholders with money, which was much needed; and, started off, therefore, one morning, with Lieut. Cuthbert, the Royal Artillery, and Lieutenant Willes, of the Fusileers. After much delay, the Siekh cavalry escort succeeded in getting their horses to swim the Goompty, which was swollen by the rains. The sun shone with all its refulgence, and raised blisters on our noses, as we passed village after village embowered in large mangoe groves, and encompassed by the long yellow crops of the season, which were moved to and fro by the high wind blowing hot in our faces. The people were timid, and distressed at the partial desertion of their companions, many of whom were fighting in the ranks of the enemy. Several complained of the licence of our cattle-drivers, who drove their animals into ripening fields, and extorted provisions, and sometimes money, to stay them from robbing. Our camp followers remorselessly plundered the helpless wherever they could reach in safety, and, such was the terror of the British arms, that the meanest fellow from the English camp could turn out a whole village to pillage their hearths! These contemptible wretches inflicted more mischief on the population of Oudh than our battles, and many an innocent family was violated and plundered by them in the name of the "Company Bahadoor."

Colonel Purnell, of the 90th Foot, commanded the

force at Nawabgunj, which was located, in thatched sheds, on a dry sandy plain, and hid in a storm of hot dust, which blew hard in our faces as we rode into the lines. I had not been there since the ride from Lucknow in June 1857, to fetch in the families from the mutinous troops at Secrora, and it pleased me now to enter the place under circumstances so much more favourable. I saw the gallant commander, and after lunching with the officers of the 23th Fusileers, and showing my wound to Dr. Sylvester, (who thought me mad for venturing out,) Cuthbert, Willes, and myself, recrossed the country to our little encampment: which we reached at night, after losing our way in the dark, and riding forty miles on a very hot day.

Our stay at Goosaingunj very much weakened the influence of the rebel leaders. They never ventured closer than fourteen miles, excepting at night, when small parties pounced on unsuspecting landholders, and either killed them, or carried them off to extort the payment of a ransom. We endeavoured, as much as possible, to check these raids, and to give confidence to the peasantry, and succeeded till reports of a threatened advance by Benee Madho emboldened the rebels, and induced the authorities to move Colonel Bulwer's force further south, to Jubrowlee, to co-operate with Brigadier Eveligh in resisting that redoubtable chief. I left Colonel Bulwer here to go into Lucknow to see my family, which had just arrived from Calcutta, and to settle them in a home till the war was over. My wife had been distressed by repeated rumours of my death, and the prognostics of friends that I could not escape the perils into which I was always rushing; and she was, therefore, glad to have occular evidence of my existance after a separation of nine months.

Before she had recovered from the joy of our meeting, an order reached me from the Chief Commissioner to proceed at once to Sundeela, where, he said, my presence with the force under Brigadier George Barker was indispensible. Previous to transporting the reader there, I will briefly tell the achievements of Bulwer's column after I was relieved by my friend Mr. James Anderson, Assistant Commissioner: one of Havelock's Volunteer Calvary, with which he did good service during the advance from Allahabad to the relief of the garrison at Lucknow.

Shortly after leaving him Colonel Bulwer had a cavalry engagement, a few miles from his camp, with the infantry of the enemy, who had no time to get away; and the spirited young Mitford, Anderson, and the Colonel, signalized themselves during the short combat, which sent over forty of the mutineers to paradise. Benee Madho, who was in the neighbourhood, excited by the British Commander's impudence, some days afterwards sent down upon him a host of foot and horse, supported by some great guns; and, as usual, they began the attack with drums and trumpets. The contending forces were very unequal in numbers, and at the beginning of the engagement one of the two English guns was disabled. The enemy blazed away at a distance, and progressed so slowly, that our small force had time to recover from its amazement; and Bulwer actively used the opportunity to feel the left flank of Benee Madho; which proved to be so weak, in all but numbers, that Cuthbert's nine-pounder and the Siekh cavalry, led on by Bulwer, Anderson, Hawkins, Mitford, (who was wounded,) and Pennington, pushed right into it. The whole mass of six thousand rebels and mutineers turned right about, and, leaving their guns behind, flew in disorder after their great leader, who went off on an elephant to extol the stratagem by which he had discovered the prowess of his army! Bulwer good naturedly accelerated their departure as much as possible, and he was afterwards the wonder of the neighbourhood, till ordered to Poorwa, on the west of the Cawnpoor road.

There Benee Madho, reinforced by about fourteen thousand infantry, a second time cautiously attacked him in the front, and on both flanks, with three separate columns. The British leader had now more cavalry, and two guns. He patiently continued, nearly all day, the game of long bowls, at which natives are great adepts. Benee Madho, deceived by his inertness, spread out his strength to give Colonel Bulwer's force a final embrace, and obliged our two little guns to turn all round to resist his approaches, while the cavalry chased him back. At last the Colonel saw his chance, and, improving it on the right by a dashing charge of cavalry led by Lieutenant Drummond, and another on the left led by Hawkins, he crushed the spirit of the enemy, and turned their faces homewards, which they made great haste to reach with the pressing help of the victors, who triumphantly brought back two of their guns. Colonel Bulwer had the modesty not to call these "pitched battles," nor were they; but his waiting to be opposed by such enormous numbers, and his skill in successfully resisting, and then driving them back confused and dispirited, placed the two engagements among the best of the season. The calm courage and decision, the gentle temper, superior intelligence, and good practical sense of this officer, point to him as one well fitted for high command.

Oudh is divided into twelve districts. and they cover an area of about 25,000 square miles. Towards the middle of October not a fourth of the province had submitted to British rule, and it was only where the English troops were stationed that there was a semblance of authority. A few police posts had been indiscreetly pushed out here and there to reassure the people; but the enemy soon surrounded and murdered the policemen. Across the Gogra—a majestic river dividing the province in two—the rebel government reigned supreme, and affected to govern the territory through two Parliaments composed of reprobates elected by interest and bribery, who confined their parliamentary functions to enforcing payment of the land revenue in the name of the puppet King Birjis Kuddur, or of his mother the Begum, whom it never reached entire. Commissioners, and Deputy Commissioners, and Assistant Commissioners, purchased permission to administer civil and criminal justice, and, armed with mandates bearing great illegible seals, they spread over the richest towns and villages, and did justice to nobody but themselves. Military officers, and their greedy followers, were fed and enriched at the expense of the people, who, despite of all this outrageous abuse of power, managed to be the gainers, and, therefore, preferred their misgovernment to the orderly and exacting rule of the English.

On the third day after quitting the force of Colonel Bulwer, I rode thirty-six miles in the morning to the camp of Brigadier Barker, who had retired to the shade of the mangoe groves of Sundeela after driving the enemy across the Goompty. He had about 750 European Infantry and Cavalry, and 850 Native Infantry and Cavalry, with 14 guns—a force ample for the reconquest of the Western Districts of Oudh, where he had only two opponents, who stayed inside their defences at Birrwa and at Rohya. The first was held by Gholab Singh, the man that, after being defeated at Ruheemabad and Sundeela, beat Dawson back from his fort; and the second belonged to Raja Nurput Singh, who was notorious for resisting General Walpole, and killing the noble Adrian Hope. The inhabitants this side of Oudh were less hostile than elsewhere, and nearly all but those two chiefs had tendered their submission.

With the aid of Brigadier Barker I dismantled the fortresses in our neighbourhood, all of which were encompassed by broad belts of the bamboo plant that formed a beautiful impenetrable barrier. This precautionary measure greatly distressed the chiefs, as it degraded them in the eyes of their rebellious compeers, who jeered them, from across the river, for their submission to so much dishonour. Rather than endure the demolition of their forts two small chiefs deserted to the enemy, and they only returned to me on seeing that it was useless resisting a dishonour in which all the Barons of Oudh were soon involved. I also forced them to surrender as many guns as we could discover, and to pay the arrears of land revenue not already collected by the rebels.

The discontent of the Sepoys was mostly confined to young soldiers, who, having few benefits to remember, and the unsteadiness of youth to mislead them, overawed veterans that had many years eaten our salt and were looking forward to the period when the bounty of Government would enable them to settle comfortably at their homes. We were one afternoon agreeably surprised by a visit from one of the British pensioners, who was carried in a litter, and being blind and infirm, was led by me to a seat: an attention that brought tears to his eyes, and blessings on the head of the "Company Buhadoor." He uncovered his fine old head, and running his fingers through his scanty hair, pathetically told us that it was black and plentiful when he entered the service of the English: that it was grey when he left it: and that it was now falling off in a home provided by the bounty of the Government. He showed us his scars, and the fire came back to his blind eyes as he recounted, in an animated voice, the battles of the English and the noble valour of his officers. He laid great stress on the frequent bestowal of Batta, or service money, after each success, and lauded the extreme regularity and justice of the English to their soldiers. The great earnestness of the aged man rivetted our attention, and we could all have risen and embraced the honest fellow when he angrily spoke of the cowardice and ingratitude of the mutineers, and deplored the loss of honour by the army in which he had himself served nearly sixty years.

I afterwards learnt that he always spoke of his old masters with affection, and that he frequently endangered his life by condemning, to their faces, the dastardly and ungrateful behaviour of the mutineers. He drew the pension of a native officer, and being about ninty years old, his career in our service must have begun when the bold but rash Tippo Sahib was provoking Marquis Cornwallis to the war that ended in the capture of Seringapatam, the death of Tippo, and the subjection of the southern provinces of India; and it must have continued to the pursuit and destruction of the roving Maharatta robbers; to the degradation of the great Mogul at Delhi; to the forfeiture of the Gangetic provinces of Oudh; to the humiliation of the impudent little Goorkhas of Nepaul; to the desperate capture of the Fort of Bhurtpoor by Lord Combermere; to the chastisement of the Burmah savages to check their incursions for a time; and it must have closed with the year when a British Army started for Affghanistan to force a fool and a tyrant on a bold people: who killed him, compelled the army to retire, and then treacherously destroyed it in the mountain passes of Jujdulluck.

CHAPTER XXII.

Operations for the complete conquest of Oudh begun—Reconnoisance—Fort of Birrwa—The "ould Eighty-eight" won't stay behind—Gallant assault of the Rifles, the Siekhs, and the "wild Irish"—A flock of geese overpowered by the 88th—Assault on the centre building and slaughter of the rebels—Moral effect of the capture—Nurput Singh prepares his fort for resistance—Advance of Brigadiers Hale and Barker to attack him—Fort evacuated - Colonel Seymour's pursuit—Walpole and the Ghost of Adrian Hope—Return to Lucknow.

THE strategical movement of troops, which was to affect the complete subjugation of Oudh, began by the advance of a splendid column from Shahjehanpoor, under the command of Brigadier Troup, and of a smaller force from Furruckabad, under Brigadier Hale of the 82nd Foot. Both were to co-operate with Brigadier Barker in expelling the enemy from the positions held south-west of the river Gogra. To the south-east of Oudh Lord Clyde had collected a large force, with his usual train of heavy guns and baggage, preparatory to marching against the stronghold of Benee Madho, who continued to disregard the efforts of the Governor-General to save him. At Fyzabad, our most active and fortunate General Sir Hope Grant had constructed a bridge of boats across the Gogra, and he was impatiently waiting for the order to go over and attack the army of the Begum. Brigadiers Whetherall, Eveligh, and Horsford, had taken their places for the contest, and the return of the cold weather had made the troops impatient for the final trial of strength.

Brigadier Barker and myself communicated with the columns coming from the west, through Chowdry Hushmut Ali, a man whom I never found backward; through Bharut Singh, a spirited little chief who still held the fort near Birrwa where I had placed him after our repulse in August; and through Hurdeo Bux, an influential chief who, in the early days of the mutiny, risked his life and property to protect Messrs. Edwardes and Probyn when flying from the massacre of Furruckabad with their families, and never afterwards abandoned our cause. Brigadier Barker, (one of the most active and intelligent officers in the service,) was most eager to commence his share of the business, and, on receiving Lord Clyde's instructions, he lost no time in reconnoitering the Fort of Birrwa. I provided him with such plans and information as was obtainable, and it all tended to convince him that he had one of the most formidable forts in the province to capture at the very onset of the campaign. Accompanied by a strong escort he leisurely examined as much of the fortifications as were visible through the bamboo jungle, although the enemy, by opening their guns, attempted to keep him off. I had received my wound in leading an assault upon the south-western angle of the defences: now it was proposed to attack the eastern face from a small village perched on a mound, from which, we were told, the interior works could be bombarded. He made a demonstration towards the mound as if to force the enemy off; but the artifice did not dislodge them, and the Brigadier, having no wish to bring on an engagement, returned to Sundeela with two of the escort wounded.

At two o'clock the following morning, and while it

was yet dark, Brigadier Barker left Sundeela with infantry, cavalry, artillery, and sappers, to attack Birrwa. He reached it at dawn, but not before tidings of his approach had gone to Gholab Singh, who fired a salute of guns from the ramparts as the head of the column emerged from the low jungle fringing the south face of the fortress, to advise us of his determination to resist. Under shelter of the trees the troops breakfasted while the Brigadier arranged for the occupation of the mound, from which the enemy loudly challenged him to come on. At eight o'clock the Oudh Military Police, (led by Captain Dawson,) and the Rifle Brigade, (under the intrepid Major Oxenden,) were pushed across a morass for the purpose of attacking the north face of the village. A heavy fusilade from the mound was maintained at the infantry, and a couple of light guns that struggled through the water; but, as soon as they crossed it, the enemy slackened fire, and on observing some of them in full retreat towards the fort, I ventured to gallop into the village alone. The sight of a mounted Englishman, armed with a long sword, very much quickened their flight. The Rifles at once turned into the village, and the Brigadier searched in vain for the spot from whence he was to see the interior of the defences. Nothing but a green flag rising above the foliage of the bamboos was visible, which indicated the position of the fort, and served as a guide for the officer at the mortars.

The 88th Regiment was advanced to the south through high cultivation, and I was galloping across to a small party fearlessly pushing straight up to the outer works, when my attention was attracted to two privates who ran panting at the tail of my Arab.

"Your regiment is behind men, and why are you leaving it? You will get into trouble."

"Divil a bit we care yer honor!" answered one of them with a good Hibernian accent. "Don't ye see the Rifles ahead, and the 'ould eighty-eight' ain't going to stay behind 'em! Surely ye won't mind our sticking up for the karacter o' the regiment?" And right well Sullivan and Malone did it, for throughout the day these gallant fellows kept in the front doing excellent service by "falling for the inimy," as they said: and a very nasty feeling it doubtless was, to judge from the bloody effects of it.

The Rifles were sent down from the mound, through a splendid grove of trees, to the verge of the bamboo belt, where only a few yards of the south-west bastion of the inner fort were faintly visible. Dawson, with his Siekhs, was on the left, and the horse artillery, and 88th Foot, were on the right. With extraordinary boldness Brigadier Barker pushed up his eight-inch howitzer, and an eighteen-pounder gun, to within a hundred yards of the bastion, trusting to the cover afforded to the gunners by the jungle. The Siekhs crouched along to the north gate, which the enemy kept open for escape when in peril. Major Maynard, with his desperate Irishmen, gradually worked round to the point attacked by me in August, and thereby secured access to the eastern gate of the outer works. The rebels were a thousand strong in the morning, but in the afternoon it was clear, from the diminished resistance, that the faint-hearted had gone off through the jungle that extended for miles to the north and completely checked any attempt at pursuit. About two o'clock P.M. the noisy cheers of the 88th were heard eastward, and soon after the Brigadier learnt that they had effected a lodgment in the outer defences, and driven the enemy to the inner work: which was protected by a great ditch forty feet across, and thirty-five feet in depth, with water in some places.

The breach in the bastion being practicable by three o'clock, a storming party was formed, with a reserve, by the Rifle Brigade, and the Punjab Sappers carried the ladders. Lieutenant Carnegie, of the Bengal Engineers, was deputed to blow open the eastern gate, and Captain Dawson, of the Military Police, was instucted to seize the north escape, and prevent the rebels getting away through the jungle. The assault was admirably managed, and, in a few minutes, the breach was mounted, the gates forced, and the enemy driven into a large house in the centre of the fort, and cut off from every chance of escape. Major Maynard was met by a discharge of grape. Captain Carnegie succeeded in nailing a powder bag to the gate: thinking the fuse had failed, he intrepidly returned with a lighted port fire, and reached just as the powder exploded, shattering the gate to pieces and burning him in a frightful manner. He was so blackened that the assaulting party mistook him for a native as they rushed through the ruins, and he narrowly escaped being bayonetted! Ensign Richards, of the Rifles, was first in at the breach, and dangerously wounded; Major Goodenough followed, and was shot in the hand; Serjeant Malony, of the Rifle Brigade, and the assaulting party, with difficulty clambered after them through the rubbish, for the ladders proved to be too short for the ascent. Lieutenant Alexander, who commanded the storming party, came back with an arrow in his shoulder. Dawson reached the north escape in time to drive back the rebels, who got jambed in the gateway by their too great eagerness to get away.

Darkness was approaching, and the cavalry posted outside the jungle had no chance of meeting any of the rebels. The noise and confusion within the fort grew awful as all the assailants pressed in to crush the desperate men in the doomed house, from which the unfortunate wretches kept up a fatal fire through loopholes. The Brigadier sheltered his men, and was making arrangements to blow in the east wall of the house, when the Irish broke loose in chase of a flock of geese, and did not return to their places till all the birds were caught and many of the pursuers killed! After this excitement had subsided, the Brigadier was importuned by Captain Dawson to let him go into the house with his Siekhs and finish the day's business. He thanked Dawson for the proposal, but declined to expose him to certain death: for the building just then could only be entered by a window little more than two feet square. The Chief turned to attend to the work of the engineers, and was immediately pulled round by the cheering of the men, which was excited by Captain Dawson's passage through the window! Knowing the cruel fate that Dawson was recklessly braving, he called to the soldiers to follow him quickly; and a Rifleman reached in time to save Dawson: who scrambled out with one arm nearly off, while his saviour hopelessly struggled inside a narrow dark passage and was cut to pieces! The arm was amputated, and Dawson died soon after a victim to his own rashness.

The straw along the roof was set fire to, and the flames drove the defenders to the lower rooms, in which they were closely packed, when the barrels of powder piled against the east wall exploded with a tremendous crash, and filled the yard with the ruins. It was now dark. With loud cheers the assaulting party entered the inner apartments, stepping over the bodies of the rebels killed by the explosion, and fearlessly encountering the survivors in the midst of the burning building, where a horrid scene of carnage terminated the fight. Gholab Singh, the leader, and five more, escaped to an inner room, and there resolutely defended themselves. The Brigadier withdrew his soldiers from the house, and left the defenders to be devoured by the flames fast spreading to the apartment. At midnight he returned to Sundeela with all but the 88th Foot, and a regiment of Military Police, which were left under the command of Major Boileau, Commandant of Police, who was present rendering good service throughout the attack. After warning the sentries to prevent the escape of Gholab Singh, he rested by my side on the floor of a cold room, and was talking of the gallantry that had captured so strong a fortress in eight hours, when we were called to arms by the rapid discharge of musketry. On running to the spot we discovered that Gholab Singh had suddenly dashed through the guards, leaped forty feet from the top of the nearest bastion to the bottom of a dry ditch, and escaped to the jungle! Two of his companions were suffocated in the burning room: two more were killed in the desperate leap: and only one accompanied Gholab Singh in his flight. It was a gallant—a very gallant—escape, and, great as was the disappointment at losing so dangerous a leader, his courage was highly extolled, and I could not lament his flying from the dreadful fate that awaited him. He was of humble origin, but shrewd and unscrupulous. The widow of the Chief of Birrwa had admired his manly proportions, and admitted him to her confidence. He assumed the management of her affairs, and, at last, ruled as lord over all. He afterwards died fighting against us in the mountains of Nepaul, and thus closed a career common enough in India.

In a week the fort was levelled to the ground, and made completely indefensible by the destruction of the dense bamboo jungle around it. The capture of this important stronghold instilled fear into the rebel leaders throughout the district, and produced offers of submission from chiefs beyond it, which the generous policy of the Government empowered me to accept: for it was distinctly announced to all civil officers with troops, and to the military commanders, that it was not to be a war of retribution, and that force was only to be used when persuasion failed to procure submission to our authority.

Raja Nurput Singh, of Rohya, was the only Talookdar who rejected our pacific overtures, and he sent me word, by a spy, that he was in the hands of the mutineers, and powerless to accept them, supposing he could credit our forgiveness of the death of so many English soldiers in the ditch of his fortress. The influence he gained by that disaster was mildly exercised, and his part of the rebellious province was freer from violence than any other. Had General Walpole been more cautious there is no doubt that this man would not have had the death of so many Englishmen to frighten him from his allegiance. He was aged, and a cripple.

Nurput Singh repaired his defences, and spread it abroad that he meant to die within them rather than surrender. He had 1200 infantry, and about 200 cavalry, and eight guns were mounted on the ramparts. Brigadier Hale, from Furruckabad, forced the rebels from Sandee, and he was advancing towards Rohya when Brigadier Barker broke ground at Sundeela, and, leaving a police regiment behind to guard the stores, marched onward to meet him. On the afternoon of the second day he halted within seven miles of Rohya, and I sent in the last invitation to Nurput Singh to surrender. No answer was returned. In the morning Brigadier Hale approached from the west, and Brigadier Barker advanced to a large village south of the fort, where they were to concert a plan of attack, and begin the bombardment. Within three miles of Rohya a revenue defaulter, in irons, informed us that Nurput Singh, leaving his prisoners behind, had evacuated the fort during the night, and gone to the north with all his guns and treasure! We galloped forward to see if it was so, and were only stopped at the gate by a flock of geese, which were soon fastened to the saddles of our escort. A few miserable villagers vanished through the opposite gate on hearing us approach. The Bays and Police Cavalry, under Colonel Seymour, were sent in pursuit of Nurput Singh; and, after being out all day, returned without discovering his track, for the villagers pretended ignorance or endeavoured to mislead him. The country for nearly twenty miles was so covered by brush wood that he could make no progress without guides, while it afforded superior cover for the retreat of the enemy.

I rode *over the walls* up to the ruined citadel, and, on turning round, was amazed that so defenceless a place shculd hove cost so many precious lives when General Walpole attacked it. All the angry feelings that disaster then provoked in the Highland brigade, were revived in us, as we examined the spot where Adrian Hope fell. Brigadier Barker set fire to the thatched houses within the enclosure, and the flames and smoke being seen by Brigadier Hale, he hurried forward to learn the cause, and an hour after the two commanders united and encamped together, and those interchanges of hospitality begun which are the delight of British officers when the fortunes of war bring them together. Mr. R. Berkely, (one of the best uncovenanted civilians in the Oudh Commission), accompanied the Furruckabad column, and we lost no time in beginning an acquaintance which I hope to renew on my return to India, for his social virtues are good as his official qualities.

A copy of the Queen's proclamation assuming the administration of India and abolishing the cumberous rule of the Court of Directors, was forwarded to me, in a sealed packet, to be opened on the 1st of November and read to the troops. Mr. Berkeley and myself, through the chiefs present, summoned the surrounding landholders to witness the interesting ceremony of turning out an old and substituting a new government destined to effect many remarkable changes in the condition of India. What a pity it is that so much of the old leaven has been left to sour the new mould! The wonderful rise of the British empire under the rule of the Court of Directors imparted a grandeur to the poor old men who were to be discharged for too obstinately adhering to the traditions of the Company; and, if they had not behaved so shabbily to me,* I might have felt some remorse at proclaiming their degradation.

On the morning of the 1st of November the troops

* When I was recommended for the Victoria Cross by Lord Canning, these gentlemen declined to forward the proposal to Her Majesty's Government, and thought it would soothe me to learn that "Mr. Kavanagh would be entitled to the medal which they anticipate Her Majesty will confer upon the garrison and relieving army of Lucknow!" Men who could think that a silver medal was enough for the services rendered by me at the relief of Lucknow, *must* have been unfit to govern an empire.

paraded, and the Proclamation was read. Three hearty cheers were given for the Queen—a right good Queen!—a royal salute was fired from eighteen-pounder guns that boomed the tidings many miles away—the National Anthem was played by all the bands—and the arms of our Most Excellent Sovereign displaced those of the defunct Court: which no one present regretted. Translations of the Proclamation were eagerly accepted by the people, who despatched them to their friends in the camp of the enemy, and the good effect of the gracious terms of peace offered in the name of Her Majesty soon manifested itself. The people never understood how the government of India was administered in England, and the corporate designation of the "Company Buhadoor," was most perplexing to them. Although somewhat amused at the idea of being ruled by a Lady, the fact was comprehensible, and carried in it a power with which they could not invest a company of merchants.

There being nothing more for the troops to do in this direction, my place with the force was taken by Major J. Carnegie, the Deputy Commissioner of the District; and I was directed to remain at Sundeela, to disarm the people, to demolish fortifications of every kind, and to proceed with the summary settlement of the land revenue. I was only there a couple of days when I was urgently called into Lucknow to see my wife, who was said to be dying.

CHAPTER XXIII.

Fort of Mythowlie and its infamous Chief—Heroic death of Captain P. Orr—Ordered to Nawabgunj-Burabunkee—The enemy frightened—A fortunate General terrifies Benee Madho from his Fort—Benee Madho puzzled—Major Gall's attempt to escape with a despatch—Benee Madho's defeat and invisible flight—No more fighting—Wonderful escape of Prince Feroze Shah—Lord Clyde and the end of the War.—Adieu!

WHILE Sir George Barker and Brigadier Hale were pacifying the south-west districts, Brigadier Troup was slowly progressing in the north-west with one of the best brigades in the field, containing the 60th Rifles, come down from Delhi covered with honour; and the 93rd Highlanders, hardened by its gallant services from Lucknow to Barielly. After frightening away a large force of rebels sent out to destroy them, the brigade leisurely advanced on the Fort of Mythowlie, took a distant look at it, bombarded the place from afar, and occupied the defences as soon as the Raja had gone off with his followers.

The name of Lone Singh is doubtless familiar to the public as the chief who reluctantly sheltered in the hot wilds of his estate the English fugitives from the massacres of Seetapoor and Mahomdee, starved and degraded the sufferers, and then surrended them to the rebel government, at Lucknow, to be murdered.

The captives were dragged to the presence of the fanatic Ahmud-oolla from comfortable rooms in the Palace. Captain Patrick Orr, (an amiable and intelligent officer well known in Oudh,) was among the prisoners, and the Moulvie promised him his life if he would disclose the name of the person who made their captivity so pleasant. "I cannot tell!" was the prompt reply. "But you shall!" angrily exclaimed the monster, as he broke the foot of the Englishman by a pistol-shot. A look of defiance was shot back, and immediately the captives were savagely despatched without a murmur, for they were prepared for a fate every day threatened since their surrender by the Raja of Mythowlie: who has, himself, recently pined away and died in captivity.

Lord Clyde stayed at Allahabad till the issue of the Queen's proclamation, when he made a long ride with his staff across to the force destined to subdue the south-eastern districts. A powerful body of rebels and mutineers were assembled under the chief of Amethee, who stayed behind the walls of his very formidable fort; and by the notorious Benee Madho, who called his followers around him with the avowed intention of resisting to the utmost, and of dying in the cause of the King to whom he had sworn allegiance, if unsuccessful. The Commander-in-Chief would not hurry, in order that the proclamation might have time to reach and be understood by the rebels, to whom it offered a free pardon, excepting murderers and the vilest leaders. The Raja of Amethee, after saving his honour by shooting at the advance guard, concealed his best guns, let all his armed followers escape through the jungle, and then surrendered on the most favourable terms of the proclamation. The honest frankness of the British

Chief subserved the artifice of the native Baron, who, however, was somewhat repentant of his success when the wrathful voice of Lord Clyde thundered in his ears. Sir Hope Grant could not overtake the fugitives from the fort, and the troops afterwards advanced, in separate columns, to engage Benee Madho in the fort of Shunkerpoor.

On my return to Lucknow from Rohya I was installed in the office of Civil Judge, to be near my wife during her illness. The war had stifled all disputes pending at the first outbreak of the mutiny, and every vestige of them, in the form of volumnious records, were destroyed when we took shelter in the Residency. The commercial business of the city was commencing to recover from the effects of the two sieges, and the litigious spirit of the people from the terrible pressure of the times, when this court was re-established on a system entirely different from the dilatory and expensive one in use before the mutiny.

On the 8th of November I entered upon my new duties, but five days later the exigences of the service rendered a change of civil officers at Lucknow necessary, and I was ordered to join Brigadier Purnell's brigade at Nawabgunj on the road to Fyzabad. The enemy had been driven from this town in June, and a force stationed there, and twenty-five miles further on at Duriabad, to preserve the communication of Sir Hope Grant when he moved on to Fyzabad. Both columns were to act on the defensive, and only attack the enemy when they ventured too close. The 1st Bengal Fusileers, under Brigadier Sir John Seaton, and the levy of the Raja of Kupoortulla, on two occasions distinguished themselves by making long marches under a scorching sun, and driving the enemy, with great slaughter, into the river Gogra. But the brigade at Nawabgunj did nothing of that sort, and the rebels, therefore, encamped within seven miles in an immense wilderness of low brushwood, and destroyed a police station imprudently pushed out too far. The troops were in excellent health, but dispirited at their inactivity, which had caused them to be spoken of as the dullest force in Oudh; and they were anxiously looking for their share of the grand winter campaign begun across the Goompty, from which the report of guns was occasionally wafted to increase their ardour. My arrival in the camp was supposed to portend active proceedings. I was assailed with numerous questions, and my inability to satisfy the curious was attributed to political reticence. I believe there was some hope among the civilians in Lucknow that my impetuosity would commit Brigadier Purnell to a fight for the wilderness; but he was too cautious an officer to be led beyond his instructions, and it was to no purpose that I galloped about, like Puss in great boots, armed with a long sabre.

The day after my arrival a strong detrachment, under the command of the Hon. Major Burke, of the 88th Foot, went out to Buttai, a large village which the enemy occupied at night and quitted in the morning; and, on our advancing, to the high ground beyond it, drums and bugles sounded in the jungle, and retreating cavalry vanished behind the foliage of the trees. Major Burke consented to take his troops further on, and, as we halted on the plain, rebels and mutineers—foot and horse—advanced to the edge of the forest, and screamed defiance at us. About two hundred British infantry, and a hundred and fifty cavalry, stood a quarter of a mile off, quietly gazing at some twelve thousand opponents! The jungle swarmed with armed men, and two little guns opened on us with no effect, and two thousand irregular cavalry kicked up a great dust as they galloped to the front only to add to the picturesque effect of the groups fringing the jungle. While the troops halted and joked at the commotion they had created, I ventured to ride within musket range towards the native cavalry, hoping to draw some of them after me. I shook my fist at the fellows, and tried to provoke them out; but only the infantry left their cover, and a few discharges from Major Burke's two nine-pounder guns soon drove them back.

The 2nd Dragoon Guards would have been glad of an opportunity of crossing swords with the horsemen in the jungle, had they shown a disposition to engage them a second time. When the enemy first began to occupy the jungle, cavalry patrols went out daily, and, on one of those occasions, Captain Powell pursued some match-lock-men into a village; and, being unable to dislodge them, set fire to the houses. Under cover of the jungle the 12th regiment of irregular cavalry surprised the Bays, who retreated at full speed till a favourable distance from the jungle was reached, when the gallant Powell turned his squadron sharply round, dashed into the midst of them, and inflicted such havoc, that the survivors lost no time in getting away. With this mishap fresh in their memories it was not surprising that the 12th and 15th Irregular Horse did not respond to my advances. I rejoined our bold little detachment as they marched back to their encampment after frightening the poor wretches in the wilderness, who were doubtless glad to see them depart. Their guns fired long after we were out of sight.

Lord Clyde was a very fortunate General, for he despatched all his foes without fighting them. His renown was enough to overthrow the redoubtable Benee Madho, and, when his Lordship reached the fort of Shunkerpoor, it was empty. It was no bad thing to have terrified two great chiefs out of the strongest forts in Oudh, albeit that His Excellency's ravenous army thought it a shame that the rebels were let do such sensible things. Benee Madho was puzzled where to go, owing to the admirable arrangements of the Commissioner-in-chief leaving him few chances of escaping. The road from Lucknow to Cawnpoor was well guarded on the west; on the east Sir Hope Grant, Brigadier Horsford, and other Commanders pressed him; on the north he would have to break through the troops at Nawabgunj and Duriabad; and to the south he might be drowned in the river Ganges: and thither he went, impelled by necessity and not by any liking for the waters of the sacred river, which the rains had swollen to a great depth. Benee Madho moved, however, so quickly, and our information came so lowly, that he very much bothered the Generals, who spread their splendid Brigades over the country in the hope of catching him somewhere. Many of his followers dispersed, and either went to their homes, or hid themselves in the great jungles running along the river Goompty and there waited for an opportunity of escaping across the Fyzabad road to the army of the Begum beyond the river Gogra.

The tidings brought through our spies from that direction, and pressing messages from Lucknow, put our column at Nawabgunj on the alert; and a portion was taken out at night, by Brigadier Purnell, to intercept Benee Madho. In the morning a cavalry escort went out with Lieutenant Palmer and myself, and returned from the Goompty in the evening, with intelligence that the rebels in the jungle were being pressed by Brigadier Horsford, and were likely to cross us during the night. A party of native regular cavalry, with an elephant, said to be carrying the family of Benee Madho, did pass towards morning, and, in attempting to pursue them, we separated from our artillery, and lost our way in the dark. We remained out two days under shelter of the trees, and then marched disappointed back to Nawabgunj, the soldiers letting out their chagrin in extempore ditties something like this:—

Where have you been to all the day
  Benee Madho, Benee Madho?
Trying to keep, sir, out of the way,
  Very bad O! very bad O!
Why so shy of British pluck
  Benee Madho, Benee Madho?
Because to beat you isn't my luck,
  That's very sad O! very sad O!

The most contradictory accounts reached us of the doings of the Commander-in-Chief, and we went out of Nawabgunj, almost every day, only to return in time to let the rebels go by. The rascals in the Buttai jungle once brought the Brigadier back by threatening to fall on our standing camp, which a spirited foe could easily have reached and burnt down in an hour.

Lord Clyde pressed on from Shunkerpoor to the town of Roy Bareilly, where Major Gall was killed at the commencement of the mutiny in attempting to escape to Allahabad, in disguise, with a despatch for the Governor-General of India from Sir Henry Lawrence. He imprudently halted with his small cavalry escort at an inn, and while refreshing himself, he was discovered, and, deserted by his native comrades; he is said to have shot himself to escape from the savage wretches who attacked him. Brigade Eveligh watched Benee Madho while Lord Clyde pushed on by forced marches towards Dhoondia Khera, where the distressed chief stopped, with the Ganges rolling fiercely behind him, and a disheartened force that had dwindled down from twenty-five to twelve thousand men. The British army advanced to engage him in good spirits, and the high crops and woods were soon enveloped in smoke, as Lord Clyde led his troops forward to the centre, and Eveligh to the right flank of the rebels. The terrified creatures gave way and followed the course of the river with our cavalry and artillery, trying to overtake them. Some were killed and a few drowned, but Benee Madho got away with his treasure to the north of the Gogra, leaving almost the whole of the country south, or more than half of the province to be peacably settled by the Civil officers.

Lord Clyde next concentrated his troops at Lucknow, and Sir Hope Grant made his arrangements at Fyzabad for crossing over the Gogra to the Begum. I was suddenly called into Lucknow to go with Brigadier Eveligh to reduce the Chief of Mohan, who still remained in a fort nineteen miles north of Lucknow. But this arrangement was altered, and I was directed to proceed with Mr. William Forbes, Commissioner, seventy miles from Lucknow to Seetapoor, from which the enemy had just been expelled by Brigadier Troup. I was now to return the sword to its scabbard; to discharge my revolver; and to draw forth from the desk the quill that had lain dry for nearly eighteen months. I did not like the change while the din of war was yet in my ears, and the gay scarlet-coated troops not gone from my sight; and I pined for a chance of escaping the drudgery of an office till peace and quietness returned to the province. My superiors, however, thought I had had enough of the danger and excitement of war, and they took the first opportunity of placing me where my civil experience would be useful.

The road to Seetapoor was not open, and we therefore proceeded to the camp of Brigadier Eveligh, which was on the road to Seetapoor. The chief of Mohan wounded seventeen of the 5th Fusileers, and escaped through the jungle to a ferry on the Gogra, and Engineers were busy destroying his wretched little fort when we reached the camp and threw ourselves on the hospitality of the officers of the 2nd Battalion of the Rifle Brigade, who needed no pressing to be kind to way-worn travellers. Two days after, Mr. Forbes, Captain Thompson, and myself, rode alone, about twelve miles across country, to ascertain whether the road to Seetapoor was safe, and, fortunately for us, we turned back within a few miles of the town of Barec, through which Prince Feroze Shah was then passing in full flight towards central India. The movements of Brigadiers Troup and Barker had driven this Delhi prince to the Gogra, and while they were rejoicing at their success, Feroze Shah suddenly broke through them with fifteen hundred cavalry, and executed the boldest feat of the war. In the face of three British columns he marched over a hundred miles through Oudh, crossed two rivers, and was only overtaken at the Jumn, eighty miles further on, by the most extraordinay exertions, and there he only lost his women and baggage.

Lord Clyde crossed the Gogra at Fyzabad, and skillfully drove the enemy into the inhospitable forests at the foot of the Himalaya mountains, where they vainly resisted for a time. Ultimately, many threw away their arms and retired to their homes, some surrendered, and the remainder retreated to the hills with the odious Nana of Bithoor, Benee Madho, and other leaders; where they were let stay till cold and starvation diminished their ardour, when Jung Buhadoor easily vanquished the hopeless wretches.

And thus ended the most remarkable storm that England has ever encountered within her foreign possessions. Although utterly unprepared and completely surprised, her gallant sons have issued victorious from a most unequal contest. Whether engaged singly or together they maintained the glory of England; and they have fortunately preserved a magnificent Empire to a nation best able and most willing to recover it from the degradation of former misrule. It may be a happy event for the future welfare of India. If its Governors will shut their ears to the earnest warnings of the "oldest inhabitant," and will lay strong hold of the present opportunity, good fruit will spring from the soil moistened by the blood of the victims of the war.

I left India in May, 1859, and, by the time this little book is in the hands of the reader, I shall probably be on my way back, reluctantly to resume my duty under a Government that thinks me undeserving of honour, and to labor hard in a climate from which I cannot hope to escape again to Europe. For the civilities received in England and Ireland, I return most hearty thanks. To those persons who have honored me with their friendship, I can only say that the remembrance of their sympathy is all I have to take back to solace me in the sunny land of the East.